Essential
Mexico

by Fiona Dunlop

Fiona Dunlop has indulged her parallel tastes
for the tropics and for developing countries
by writing AA Explorer guides on Singapore
& Malaysia, Indonesia, Vietnam, Costa Rica,
Mexico and India. During a 15-year sojourn
in Paris she wrote *Explorer Paris* as well
as working in and covering the arts scene
for numerous publications. She is now based
in London.

Above: *the much-loved traditional* mariachi *band is found
all over Mexico*

AA Publishing

Above: *image of the Virgin of Guadalupe, Mexico City*

Front cover: *Baja California sunset; Indian weaving; a Totonac* Voladore
Back cover: *jalapeño peppers*

Written by Fiona Dunlop

Produced by AA Publishing.
© Automobile Association Developments Ltd 1999
Maps © Automobile Association Developments Ltd 1999
Reprinted Aug 2000

Distributed in the United Kingdom by AA Publishing,
Norfolk House, Priestley Road, Basingstoke, Hampshire,
RG24 9NY.

A CIP catalogue record for this book is available from the
British Library.

ISBN 0 7495 1920 7

Published by AA Publishing, a trading name of Automobile
Association Developments Limited, whose registered
office is Norfolk House, Priestley Road, Basingstoke,
Hampshire, RG24 9NY.
Registered number 1878835.

Find out more about
AA Publishing and the
wide range of services
the AA provides by
visiting our web site at
www.theaa.co.uk

Colour separation: Pace Colour, Southampton
Printed and bound in Italy by Printer Trento S.r.l.

Contents

About this Book

KEY TO SYMBOLS

✚ map reference to the maps found in the What to See section

✉ address or location

☎ telephone number

🕐 opening times

🍴 restaurant or café on premises or near by

Ⓜ nearest underground train station

🚌 nearest bus/tram route

🚉 nearest overground train station

⛴ ferry crossings and boat excursions

✈ travel by air

ℹ tourist information

♿ facilities for visitors with disabilities

✋ admission charge

↔ other places of interest near by

❓ other practical information

➤ indicates the page where you will find a fuller description

---

Essential *Mexico* is divided into five sections to cover the most important aspects of your visit to Mexico.

Viewing Mexico pages 5–14
An introduction to Mexico by the author.
   Mexico's Features
   Essence of Mexico
   The Shaping of Mexico
   Peace and Quiet
   Mexico's Famous

Top Ten pages 15–26
The author's choice of the Top Ten places to see in Mexico, listed in alphabetical order, each with practical information.

What to See pages 27–90
The five main areas of Mexico, each with its own brief introduction and an alphabetical listing of the main attractions.
   Practical information
   Snippets of 'Did you know…' information
   3 suggested walks
   4 suggested tours
   2 features

Where To... pages 91–116
Detailed listings of the best places to eat, stay, shop, take the children and be entertained.

Practical Matters pages 117–24
A highly visual section containing essential travel information.

Maps
All map references are to the individual maps found in the What to See section of this guide.
For example, Palenque has the reference ✚ 73E1 – indicating the page on which the map is located and the grid square in which the archaeological site is to be found. A list of the maps that have been used in this travel guide can be found in the index.

Prices
Where appropriate, an indication of the cost of an establishment is given by **£** signs:

£££ denotes higher prices,
££ denotes average prices, while
£ denotes lower charges.

Star Ratings
Most of the places described in this book have been given a separate rating:
✪✪✪ Do not miss
✪✪ Highly recommended
✪ Worth seeing

Viewing
Mexico

Above: *a cactus blooms in the Baja California desert*
Right: *a pilgrim advances towards the Basílica de Guadalupe*

Fiona Dunlop's Mexico

NAFTA

In 1994 Mexico, the USA and Canada inaugurated the North American Free Trade Agreement (NAFTA). This momentous economic union is designed to gradually break down all trade barriers between the three countries over a 15-year period, and has already produced an influx of American capital, particularly in the Cancún area, and in new services in the northern cities. Mexico is certainly benefiting from it economically, with 80 per cent of its exports heading north, but it is questionable how positive the long-term cultural effects will be.

Shoeshiners are part of the zócalo picture in every Mexican town

Travelling through Mexico is a strangely familiar experience, not just because I've been there before, but because so much of it has clear European and North American influences. But behind this hybrid façade lies the more secret life of the indigenous people, whose ancestors erected the most incredible pyramids and structures, observed and worshipped the stars, and were playing around with the concept of zero some 1,500 years ago while Europe was still lost in the Dark Ages.

Traditional crafts reflect the imagination and flair of the Mexicans, whether intricate handweavings, touchingly crude Tarahumara animal carvings, exquisite ceramics and silverware, or tin *milagros* (votive offerings to saints). Indigenous men and women cling to their traditional dress, with endless extraordinary regional variations. But far from being a picture of a tranquil, time-honoured existence, these people continue to suffer at the hands of landowners and political interests, a fact that visitors will become aware of.

Then there is Mexico's magnificent Spanish heritage, one of dazzling baroque masterpieces and grid-like urban layouts. The inevitable zócalo, the social crossroads of every town, is the shoeshiners' workplace and for me, the smell of shoe-polish can only mean Mexico. In contrast, as the northern border draws closer, there is a distinct feel of growing prosperity and increasing Americanisation. But this doesn't mean that *ahorita* means anything other than 'in a short while'. Long may it continue!

Mexico's Features

Geography
• Mexico's total area is 1,958,201sq km, about a quarter of the size of the USA.
• The highest peak is the Pico de Orizaba (5,700m).
• Mexico City lies at an altitude of 2,300m.
• Mexico's coastline totals 10,150km.
• Mexico is home to nearly 30,000 species of flowering plants, 1,000 species of birds, 2,000 of fish and about 450 of mammals.

Socio-economic
• Mexico is the world's most populous Spanish-speaking country.
• The population is 93 million, with over 20 million inhabiting the capital.
• The indigenous population is estimated to be nearly 30 million.
• 56 indigenous languages survive.
• 89.7 per cent of Mexicans are Catholics.
• An estimated 45 million Mexicans live in conditions of extreme poverty.
• Half a million Mexicans were arrested in 1996 while attempting to cross illegally into the USA.
• The PRI (Partido Revolucionario Institucional), the world's longest governing 'democratic' party, has clocked up over 70 years of continuous rule.

Various
• There are 200 or so varieties of chilli.
• 87 per cent of Mexico's tequila exports go to the USA.
• *Pulque*, a pre-Hispanic beer brewed from the maguey plant, still represents about 10 per cent of Mexico's total alcohol consumption.

Indigenous People
The majority of Mexicans are *mestizos*, mixed Spanish and Mexican blood, with pure indigenous groups concentrated mainly in the south, in Oaxaca, Chiapas and the Yucatán peninsula. Other pockets are found in Michoacán (Tarascans), in the mountains of Nayarit and Tabasco (Huichols) and in the rugged northern canyons (Tarahumara).

The source of pulque, mezcal *and* tequila: *the blue maguey or agave plant*

Essence of Mexico

Few nations can rival Mexico's turbulent history, and few can claim such a cultural diversity. From the enigmatic giant heads of the Olmecs and the baroque outpourings of the Spaniards, to the stark clean lines of contemporary architecture and time-honoured skills of craftspeople, Mexico proudly displays a richly creative pulse. Reflecting this are the contrasts of the land itself – tropical rainforests in Chiapas, desert in Baja California, volcanoes and lakes in the centre and *cenotes* (sinkholes) in the Yucatán. It is a country that excites, stimulates and awes: surprises lurk around every corner.

Above: *a Toltec warrior at Tula*
Right: *detail of Quetzalcóatl, the plumed serpent god*

Below: *strumming mariachis in their home town of Guadalajara*

THE **10** ESSENTIALS

If you only have a short time to visit Mexico, or would like to get a really complete picture of the country, here are the essentials:

- **Steep yourself** in colonial history in Mexico City's Centro Histórico, paying homage to the last remnants of the proud Aztec culture at the Templo Mayor (➤ 39), before retreating to a restaurant to sample pre-Hispanic cuisine.
- **Indulge in countless varieties** of tequila at the Plaza Garibaldi in Mexico City, while being serenaded by *mariachi* sounds. Do the same thing in Guadalajara (➤ 44), where the *mariachis* have their origins, or in Veracruz (➤ 81), where the *marimba* joins the band.
- **Stretch out on a Pacific beach** under a shady *palapa* at Huatulco, Puerto Escondido or Puerto Vallarta, or swim with pelicans and whales in Baja California.
- **Visit an indigenous village** in Chiapas, such as San Juan Chamula (➤ 79), to see a unique synthesis of ancient Maya worship and Catholic rituals.
- **Admire the prowess** of a baroque masterpiece and the fertile imagination of its sculptors in Taxco, Puebla, Cuernavaca, Querétaro or Oaxaca.
- **Explore the markets** of towns such as Pátzcuaro (➤ 46) or Oaxaca (➤ 72), where the craft work is outstanding, then tour the surrounding villages to observe craftspeople at work.
- **Take a boat tour** on a lagoon to observe Mexico's rich bird life, both native and migratory, at San Blas (➤ 67).
- **Get a close-up** on one of Mexico's seismic giants: Popocatépetl, neighbouring Iztaccíhuatl, Pico de Orizaba, or the Cofre de Perote, near Jalapa.
- **Explore a less-visited** archaeological site such as Yagul (➤ 76) to soak up pre-Hispanic history without the crowds.
- **Go scuba diving or snorkelling** at Cozumel (➤ 87) or Isla Mujeres (➤ 88) in the company of technicoloured tropical fish.

Products of the land range from a shot of tequila to a tantalising choice of tropical fruits

The Shaping of Mexico

60000–8000 BC
Waves of nomadic hunters cross the Bering Strait from Mongolia and gradually move south.

***c*1200 BC–AD 100**
Development of the Olmec culture along the Gulf of Mexico is followed by the Zapotecs at Monte Albán, the rise of El Tajín and, at the beginning of the Christian era, of Teotihuacán.

600–900
Zenith of Mayan culture stretching from the Yucatán peninsula to Guatemala. End of the

Classic period between the 9th and 10th centuries; rise of the Toltecs at Tula and Mixtecs in Oaxaca.

1400s
Aztecs dominate the heart of Mexico.

1502–20
Rule of Moctezuma II from the Aztec capital, Tenochtitlán (today's Mexico City).

1519
Hernán Cortés lands near Veracruz and marches on the Aztec capital.

The Spanish invaders lusted for gold

1521
The Aztec capital finally falls and Moctezuma's successor, Cuauhtémoc, is captured and killed three years later.

1535
Spanish vice-regal system is set up. Spread of the *encomienda* system (vast tracts of land given to conquerors) and virtual Indian slavery.

1767–1804
Expulsion of the Jesuits: the remaining Catholic Church is Mexico's greatest landowner. Expropriation of all Church property in 1804 leads to chaos.

1810–20
Miguel Hidalgo calls for independence, sparking off a popular revolt. Mexico City falls to the insurgents in 1820.

1821
Mexico is granted independence from Spain under a constitutional monarchy. General Iturbide declares himself Emperor, but power passes to General Santa Ana, heading a new federal republic.

1836
The cattle ranchers of Texas, enraged by the abolition of slavery, rebel and declare their independence.

1845
Texas is annexed by the United States.

1846–48
The Mexican–American War ends with a treaty that loses Mexico half its former territory.

1857
Benito Juárez instigates controversial reforms, plunging Mexico into a renewed civil war that he eventually wins in 1861. Inability to repay foreign debts leads to a joint attack by Spain, Britain and France on Veracruz. France marches on to occupy Mexico City.

1864–7
Habsburg Archduke Maximilian rules as the puppet emperor of Mexico. Juárez obtains American backing; the French withdraw.

1876–1910
Dictatorship of Porfirio Díaz rebuilds the nation at the cost of civil liberties.

1911–17
Díaz is ousted in elections by the liberal Francisco Madero, backed by revolutionary groups of Zapata and Pancho Villa. Conflicting ideals lead to civil war, with Obregón and Carranza joining attempts to dislodge the new, American-backed

President Lázaro Cárdenas

President Huerta. The revolution officially ends in 1917 with a new constitution, but conflicts continue into the 1920s.

1934–40
President Lázaro Cárdenas introduces prosperity and civil peace by redistribution of land to peasants, nationalisations and generally boosting the Mexican national identity.

1946
The ruling party since 1929 is renamed Partido Revolucionario Institucional (PRI). Corruption increases.

1988–94
The presidency of Carlos Salinas de Gortari reveals untold corruption, political assassinations, violations of human

rights, money-laundering and an increasing chasm between rich and poor.

1994
As Mexico officially enters NAFTA (North American Free Trade Agreement), a band of insurgents ('Zapatistas') takes over parts of Chiapas, demanding indigenous rights.

1995
Devaluation of the *peso* by President Ernesto Zedillo heralds Mexico's deepest recession since the 1930s.

1997
Partido de la Revolución Democrática (PRD) leader Cuauhtémoc Cárdenas is elected Mayor of Mexico City.

11

Peace & Quiet

Mexico's diverse topography, roughly categorised into three altitudes, offers a bewildering choice of escapes for those in search of a return to nature. Hand-in-hand with the rainforest, sierras, scrub, pine forests, desert and volcanic craters goes an equally varied wildlife, from iguanas, harpy eagles and quetzals to jaguars, Jesus Christ lizards and grey whales.

Savannah, Sea and Cenotes

Visitors to the Yucatán peninsula should explore the Sian Ka'an Biosphere Reserve to see the savannah edging mangrove swamps and, on the horizon, the world's second-longest ocean reef. Pumas, white-tail deer, crocodiles, howler monkeys and some 300 bird species are all resident, best observed on a trek organised through Amigos de Sian Ka'an, in Cancún. On the north and west coast respectively, Río Lagartos and Celestún reserves are favourite nesting grounds for pink flamingos, and the tiny island of Isla Contoy remains a rewarding bird sanctuary. Elsewhere in this limestone plateau, dive, swim or snorkel in one of the many *cenotes* (sinkholes).

Below: *Mexico's rich wildlife includes the hyacinth macaw*
Bottom: *the Mexican deer*

Jungle Wilds

Only about one-fifth of Mexico's original rainforest remains, mostly concentrated in Chiapas, where high rainfall helps maintain steamy jungles, much appreciated by macaws, toucans, parakeets, spider monkeys and butterflies, and mammals such as jaguars and ocelots. Montes Azules is the most accessible ecotourism destination in this region, with trips arranged from Palenque or Tenosique deep into the Lacandon Forest. Mexico's largest cloud forest is at El Triunfo Biosphere Reserve, near Tapachula in the Sierra Madre range.

Coast to Hills

Beyond the Isthmus, in the state of Oaxaca, the land becomes noticeably drier. Nature-lovers should enjoy the diving facilities at Puerto Escondido and Huatulco. Here, too, are coastal wetlands such as the Lagunas de Chacahua and the turtle sanctuary of Mazunte. In stark contrast, the area around Catemaco (southeast of Veracruz) is dubbed 'little Switzerland', while in the tiny state of Tabasco are more coastal lagoons as well as savannah and jungle.

Volcano Territory

Central Mexico is the land of the volcanoes. The national park surrounding the twin peaks of Popocatépetl and Iztaccíhuatl, the crater lakes of Nevado de Toluca, and the more strenuous ascent of Pico de Orizaba all offer extensive hiking and climbing. The Michoacán village engulfed by the seismic activity of Paricutín in the 1940s offers a striking spectacle and can be explored on a horseback tour from Uruapan. Try also the Xochimilco Ecological Park (▶ 26) on the outskirts of Mexico City.

Desert

Endless scrub, sierra and desert characterise most of northern Mexico, with notable exceptions provided by the spectacular canyons of the Sierra Tarahumara and the coastal lagoons between Mazatlán and San Blas. The biosphere reserves of the islands in the Mar de Cortés have a spectacular 570 species of plants and the sea itself over 15 species of whales and porpoises. In Baja California, the Sierra de la Gigánta and the Desierto de Vizcaíno are home to puma and lynx, as well as exceptional desert landscapes and flora.

Ecotourism
Amigos de Sian Ka'an
Cancún ☎ 98 849583

Ecogrupos de México
Mexico City ☎ 661 9121

Below: *a splash of white flowers on the Casahuata tree*
Bottom: *the dramatic volcanic lake of the Nevado de Toluca*

Mexico's Famous

*Enduring icons of
Mexican art: Diego Rivera
and Frida Kahlo*

Frida Kahlo

The darling of international feminist artists and collectors is Frida Kahlo (1907–54), the woman who battled with childhood polio, a near fatal tramway accident in her teens, and a lifetime of physical and psychological suffering to become one of Mexico's foremost 20th-century painters. Her bold images of flowers, birds and animals gradually gave way to a tortuous series of agonising self-portraits, partly stimulated by her relationship with Diego Rivera. Always extravagantly and eccentrically attired, Kahlo attended her last exhibition in Mexico City in her richest Zapotec costumes and jewellery, lying on a four-poster bed.

Diego Rivera

Variously described as an ogre, a seducer and a frog, Diego Rivera (1886–1957) is without doubt one of Mexico's greatest artistic geniuses. After indulging to the full in a decade of Bohemian life in Paris, Rivera returned to Mexico City in 1921 and began pioneering Mexican muralism, together with Orozco and Siqueiros. Much inspired by the Russian revolution, Rivera's stylised murals of class struggles, socialist ideals and the violence perpetuated against Mexico's Indians plastered government buildings all over the country. His functionalist studio in San Angel and the Museo Anáhuacalli reveal his diverse interests, but above all his passion for pre-Hispanic cultures.

Emiliano Zapata

Emiliano Zapata (1879–1919), the most charismatic figure of the Mexican Revolution, was sadly destined for a treacherous end when he was ambushed and assassinated by order of President Carranza, a former ally. Zapata's rise to revolutionary power started in 1910 when he mobilised a band of peasant insurgents in the state of Morelos with his cry 'Tierra y libertad!' ('land and freedom') and proceeded to redistribute millions of hectares of land. From his headquarters in Tlaltizapan (now a museum), Zapata led his *bandoleros* (peasant revolutionaries) into endless battles, and by 1912 controlled strategic points on the outskirts of the capital. In 1994 Zapata's name was revived by guerrilla leader Sub-Comandante Marcos to inspire a new revolt in Chiapas.

Moctezuma II

Moctezuma II, greatest of all Aztec emperors, was another of Mexico's tragic heroes. More given to meditation and learning than to warfare, he erroneously opened the doors of his palace to the Conquistadores. Convinced that Hernán Cortés was in reality the great god Quetzalcóatl returning from the east, Moctezuma showered him with priceless presents. However, even his semi-divine status among his people could not prevent him from being kidnapped by the Spaniards, or being killed.

Top Ten

Above: *Palenque's towering Templo de las Inscripciones, home to King Pakal's tomb*
Right: *a fertility goddess from Veracruz at the Museo Nacional de Antropología*

1
Barranca del Cobre
(Copper Canyon)

28B3

Daily 1st and 2nd class train leaves Los Mochis at 6AM, Chihuahua at 7AM

Airports at Los Mochis and Chihuahua

Libertad 1300, 1st Floor, Edificio Agustín Melgar, Chihuahua

Chihuahua (➤ 54)

Easter processions and dances peak on Easter Fri

Ecogrupos de México

Avenida Insurgentes Sur 1971, Colonia Guadalupe Inn, Mexico City DF 01020, organises train and trekking expeditions

(525) 661 9121. Train service (14) 109059

A rare flat stretch on the otherwise tortuous Chihuahua–Pacifico railway

Rugged canyons, spectacular waterfalls, old mining villages, Jesuit missions and the Chihuahua–Pacifico railway are the highlights here.

Five times wider and one-and-a-half times deeper than the Grand Canyon, the 35,000sq km Barranca del Cobre is rapidly becoming a major ecotourism destination. It is composed of five adjoining canyons sliced out of the Sierra Madre Occidental, their sculpted ravines offering startling extremes in climate and vegetation. In winter the upper plateau may be blanketed in snow, while on the canyon floors warm, balmy temperatures prevail; in summer the Sierra Tarahumara is refreshingly cooler than oven-like Chihuahua, though rain is abundant.

The most striking access to this region is by rail, through 88 tunnels and over 39 bridges from Los Mochis near the Mar de Cortés to Divisadero and Creel, or arriving in the other less scenic direction from Chihuahua. The main town is Creel. Facilities here include day trips on horseback or by van into the surrounding canyons, to Lago Arareco, Cascada de Cusararé, the hot springs of Recohuata or the six-hour ride to Batopilas, a former silver-mining town 2,000m below on the canyon floor. In the far north are the thundering waters of the Cascada de Basaseáchic, a 246m waterfall whose spectacular pine-clad surroundings are now a national park.

The original inhabitants of this region, the Tarahumara, now only number about 50,000. Their geographical isolation has preserved their distinctive traditions that climax during colourful Easter processions.

2
Chichén Itzá

This archaeological site is the most popular in the Yucatán peninsula. Two distinct excavated zones present extraordinary and unique structures.

Jaguar heads have surveyed Chichén Itzá for over 1,400 years

Founded in AD 514 by a priest, this ceremonial centre experienced two peaks, from 600 to 900, and again from the late 10th century until 1196. Civil wars and cultural stagnation followed before Chichén and other northern Maya civilisations finally collapsed in 1441. When the Spaniards arrived a century later, they named the partially ruined structures according to mere supposition.

At the centre of the vast plaza in the northern group rises the striking Pyramid of Kukulkán. Its 365 steps and 52 base panels represent the solar year, and twice a year, at the spring and summer equinoxes, the shadows of the north staircase create a serpentine shape that joins the carved snakes' heads at the bottom. To the northwest is a ball court, the largest yet discovered in Mexico, lined with bas-reliefs of players. Overshadowing this is the Templo de los Jaguares (Temple of Jaguars), with extensive jaguar and eagle carvings. Beside it stands the macabre Tzompantli (Platform of Skulls), that once displayed the heads of sacrificial victims.

Across the plaza is the richly decorated Templo de los Guerreros (Warriors' Temple) with, at its base, an extensive, roofless colonnade, the Mil Columnas (Thousand Columns). From the platform high above, the entire plaza is surveyed by a much-photographed *chacmool* (seated human figure).

The highlight of the older group is the Caracol (snail), an elevated circular building once used for astronomical observations. Facing it is the ornately decorated Edificio de las Monjas (nunnery) and, between them, the Iglesia (church), crowned by a remarkable roof comb and adorned with masks of the rain god, Chac.

✚ 29F2

☎ (99) 249677

🕐 Site and museum: daily 8–5; services: 8AM–10PM

🍴 Cafeteria (£)

🚌 ADO bus from Mérida, Calle 50

ℹ Tourist information offices in Mérida and Cancún

💰 Expensive; free Sun

❓ Sound and light show nightly: 8 in Spanish; 9 in English. Spring and autumn equinox celebrations

3
Guanajuato

✝ 42A2

✈ Flights from Mexico City

ℹ Plaza de la Paz 14
☎ (473) 21982

Alhóndiga de Granaditas

✉ Calle 28 de Septiembre

☎ (473) 21112

🕐 Tue–Sat 10–2, 4–6, Sun
10–3:30. Closed 25
Dec, 1 Jan, Easter Sun

*A bird's-eye view of
Guanajuato*

*Tumbling down a hillside in central Mexico
is this gem of a town. Former silver wealth
has left a legacy of superb colonial architecture.*

Historically one of Mexico's most important towns, Guanajuato originally earned its status from its rich silver mines, founded in 1546. It never looked back and in 1989 was declared a world heritage site by UNESCO. A network of underground tunnels keeps traffic out of its central plazas and alleys, making it a joy to wander in, though less so to drive in as orientation is not easy.

On a hilltop overlooking the town are the old mines of La Valenciana (one still functions), next to a 1770s church containing three fine baroque altarpieces. Further along the Carretera Panorámica is the Museo de las Momías, another of Guanajuato's unique sights, containing over 100 mummified bodies retrieved from the local cemetery where they had been impeccably preserved in the mineral-rich soil.

In the town centre, the main attraction is the **Alhóndiga de Granaditas**, which houses the regional museum. This imposing building, originally a corn exchange, played a major role in the War of Independence when it became a fortress and later the macabre showcase for the heads of captured rebels. It now exhibits pre-Hispanic objects, altarpieces, religious paintings and items related to the Independence struggle. A short walk east of here brings you to the grandiose University, one of the most important in Mexico and, just beyond, is the Templo de la Compañía de Jesús, a 1750s church with a remarkable façade. Immediately below is the focal point of town, the lively Jardín de la Unión, backed by the highly decorative Teatro Juárez.

4
Huatulco

Situated on what was once a deserted coastline, this fledgling resort offers dramatic scenery and excellent services.

Although Huatulco's string of nine bays were spotted by the Spanish conquistadores, they were never exploited as a port. For centuries, this idyllic fishing village slumbered peacefully before being earmarked in the early 1980s by Mexico's resort planners as a follow-up to Cancún. Progress was not always smooth: development suffered from the 1994–5 financial crisis and Hurricane Pauline in 1997. However, unlike other Pacific resorts, planners have learned from the mistakes elsewhere and produced an environmentally sensitive resort with low-rise hotels.

Today, Huatulco boasts an international airport, over 20 hotels, a marina, an 18-hole golf course and three developed beaches at Tangolunda (the most exclusive), Santa Cruz and Chahue, as well as a lively inland village, La Crucecita, with budget accommodation. Other beaches remain blissfully untouched with, at the most, a few *palapa* restaurants. Between the pockets of hotels are jungle-clad hills and cliffs that are rich in wildlife. Activities include jungle motorbike expeditions, kayaking, snorkelling and diving around the reefs in Huatulco's clear waters.

Although historical sights are totally absent, Huatulco boasts a modern zócalo at the centre of La Crucecita. This animated hub is overlooked by a church, **Iglesia de Guadalupe**, worth visiting for its vast contemporary mural of the Virgen de Guadalupe that decorates the entire ceiling vault.

73D1

Flights from Oaxaca, Mexico City

Boulevard Santa Cruz, corner Monte Albán, Bahía de Santa Cruz
☎ (958) 71541/2

Good

Free

Iglesia de Guadalupe

Calle Gardenia, La Crucecita

Daily 9–8

Cafés and restaurants (£–££) on plaza

Bahía Tangolunda in Huatulco, backed by the moody Sierra Madre del Sur

5
Monte Albán
(White Mountain)

Clear, high-altitude light adds to the magic of Monte Albán

'White Mountain' sits atop a levelled hill above the valley of Oaxaca. Magnificent in scale, layout and setting, it is an absolute 'must-see'.

✚ 72C1

✉ 6km west of Oaxaca

☎ (951) 64682/50002

🕐 Mon–Fri 8–5, Sat–Sun 9–3

🍴 Café (£) on site

🚌 Buses from Oaxaca, Calle Mina 518, every 30 minutes 8:30–3:30

✈ Numerous internal flights to Oaxaca

ℹ Sedetur: Independencia, corner García Vigil, Oaxaca ☎ (951) 60717

♿ Good to museum

✋ Moderate; free Sun

↔ Oaxaca (► 72)

Incredible 360-degree views of the barren hills surrounding Monte Albán give a strong sense of proximity to the gods, a fact recognised by the later Mixtecs, who used the abandoned site for offerings and burials between 1350 and the arrival of the Spaniards. The ancient Zapotec site was founded c500 BC and peaked between AD 500 and 600 with an estimated population of over 20,000. Like many other Mesoamerican sites, it was abandoned in the 8th century and, apart from its Mixtec interlude, fell into ruin.

From the site entrance and well-designed museum, a path winds uphill to the corner of the northern pyramid, where the breathtaking Gran Plaza opens up before you. To the left is a ball court, a palace and small temple platforms, and opposite are three large temple structures. Between them a 300m plaza unfolds to the majestic steps of the southern pyramid. Other buildings are aligned down the centre, yet the overall sense of space remains absolute from any vantage point.

Behind the northern pyramid are five tombs, the most elaborate being Tomb 104. East of this, near the access path, is Tomb 7, source of the fabulous Mixtec treasures displayed in Oaxaca's museum. On the western flank of the plaza, the Palacio de los Danzantes (Palace of the Dancers) was named after a series of stone slabs carved with dancing figures that stand around its base. There are countless theories about these oddly deformed figures.

6
Museo Nacional de Antropología

This museum is a must for any visitor to Mexico City, as it houses an exemplary display of the nation's indigenous cultures.

Built in the early 1960s, the Anthropological Museum does full justice to the complexities of Mexico's early civilisations through a dynamic display grouped according to regions. The focal point is a large semi-roofed courtyard fountain; surrounding it are the ground-floor galleries devoted to Mesoamerican artefacts and the upper floor to the rich diversity of surviving traditions among Mexico's indigenous populations. Another attraction is the museum's verdant location in Chapultepec Park, offering a leafy post-museum walk and plenty of local animation.

The ground-floor galleries start in the right-hand wing and follow an anti-clockwise direction around the courtyard. An introduction to world anthropology and ethnology continues with the origins of Mesoamerican man, before moving into what is termed pre-Classic civilisations (1700–200 BC). Then follow rooms dedicated to Teotihuacán, Tula (the militaristic Toltecs), México (the Aztecs), Oaxaca (Mixtecs and Zapotecs), the Gulf of Mexico (Olmecs, Huastecs and Totonacs), Maya, northern desert cultures and finally Occidente (the western cultures of Nayarit, Jalisco and Colima). A first-time visit may prove confusing, but after visiting some of the archaeological sites covered, the museum collection becomes far more relevant and illuminating.

Highlights include the giant Toltec *Atlante* statue in the Sala de Tula, the Aztec Calendar stone in the spectacular Sala México, and a huge Olmec head from San Lorenzo. Other notable exhibits are the superb Olmec *luchador* (wrestler), the Mayan mask of the Sun God, reproductions of Mayan murals from Bonampak and a reconstruction of King Pakal's tomb from Palenque.

🕇 32A2

✉ Paseo de la Reforma, corner Gandhi, Bosque de Chapultepec

☎ (553) 6381/ 6386

🕐 Tue–Sat 9–7, Sun, hols 10–6

🍴 Café (£) off courtyard

Ⓜ Chapultepec

✋ Moderate

❓ Guided tours, audio-guides, bookshop

One of the museum's treasures: a monumental Olmec head carved out of basalt

7
Palenque

The unique four-storey tower of the Palacio rises out of luxuriant vegetation

Deep in the rainforest of Chiapas stands this superb Maya site, both evocative and historically significant.

➕ 73E1

☎ (934) 50356/50211

🕐 Daily 8–5

🍴 Cafeteria (£) in museum

🚌 *Collectivo* bus to site from Calle Allende, Palenque

✈ Airstrip

ℹ Tourist office: Avenida Juárez, corner Absolo, Palenque

♿ Few

👜 Expensive; free Sun

↔ San Cristóbal (➤ 79), Tuxtla (➤ 80)

Palenque was founded in AD 615 by the great Mayan king Pakal, who set out to create a new architectural style, offering more light and harmonious, well-balanced spaces. At the centre of the main site stands the Palacio (palace), a large complex of courtyards, corridors and tunnels crowned by a tiered tower that was probably an observatory. The entire structure is decorated with relief carvings, stucco friezes and carved stelae.

Virtually opposite towers the Templo de las Inscripciones (Temple of Inscriptions), where steep steps rise to a summit temple then descend into the extraordinary tomb of King Pakal. Over 620 hieroglyphic inscriptions (including the date of 692) are surrounded by rich stucco decoration. Pakal's carved sarcophagus remains in the crypt but his fabulous jewellery is now at Mexico City's Anthropological Museum (➤ 21). Temple XIII, immediately to the west, has recently revealed the entombed body of the Reina Roja (red queen), adorned with fine jade ornaments that are at the site museum.

Across a stream on the hillside is a group of four beautiful temples. Some distance north lies another distinct group where a ball court fronts the Templo del Conde (Count's Temple). From here a path leads along the stream through jungle and past unexcavated structures to the main road and the museum and crafts shop.

8
Taxco

Taxco boasts a spectacular natural setting high in pine-clad mountains and some impressive colonial extravaganzas.

Taxco, a former staging-post on the royal road south to the port of Acapulco, developed considerably in the 18th century thanks to the enterprising French mining magnate José de la Borda, who left his mark both here and in Cuernavaca. A subsequent long and somnolent period ended in the 1930s when the American William Spratling regenerated the silver industry.

Red-roofed, whitewashed houses tumbling down the slopes line a maze of crooked cobblestoned streets winding uphill from the main road to the Plaza Borda. This social and commercial hub is overshadowed by the magnificent church of **Santa Prisca** (1759), a baroque masterpiece that was entirely financed by Borda. No expense was spared; its ornately carved façade and towers house a dazzling interior lined with 12 gilded altarpieces, oil paintings and a monumental organ.

On a tiny plaza behind the church, the Museo Guillermo Spratling exhibits pre-Hispanic artefacts and replicas. A few twisting steps downhill from here stands a museum honouring another of Taxco's illustrious foreign residents, the German explorer Baron von Humboldt, who lived here in 1803. His mansion now houses the Museo de Arte Virreinal, a beautifully presented collection of colonial art with some exceptional pieces. There are numerous other fine mansions and churches to be explored, and a lively market area in the streets below Santa Prisca, packed with silver shops, offers the joys of hard bargaining.

Finally, for panoramic views of the town from the summit of Monte Taxco, take the *teleférico* (cable-car) from Los Arcos, located on the main access road.

Looking out over the rooftops of Taxco

🕂 72C2

ℹ️ Avenida de los Plateros 1 ☎ (762) 22274

♿ Few

✋ Free

↔️ Cuernavaca (➤ 42), Acapulco (➤ 62)

❓ Easter Week processions peaking on Easter Fri

Parroquía de Santa Prisca

✉️ Plaza Borda

☎ (762) 20183

🕓 Mon–Sat 6AM–8PM, Sun 5:30AM–9PM

🍴 Cafés and restaurants (£) on square

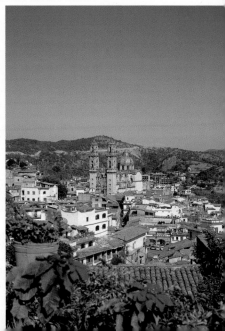

9
Teotihuacán

🕂 42C2

☎ (595) 60052

🕐 Tue–Sun 8–5

🍴 Restaurant (£) opposite the citadel

🚌 Pirámides' bus from Terminal Tapo

Ⓜ San Lázaro

ℹ️ SECTUR: Avenida Presidente Mazariyk 172, Polanco, Mexico City

🎟️ Moderate; free Sun

❓ Guided tours from Mexico City (through hotels, travel agents)

Long before the Aztecs established their capital in central Mexico, Teotihuacán was the dominant centre.

Located about one hour's drive from Mexico City, the archaeological site of Teotihuacán ('place of the dead') rises out of dry scrub and cacti. This once magnificent city, that covered over 20sq km and sustained some 85,000 inhabitants at its zenith, evolved over a period of eight centuries before its apparent destruction in around AD 750. Controversial 20th-century excavations and restoration of about 80 per cent of the structures highlight Teotihuacán's ambitious building, carving and mural techniques.

The site lies a few degrees off a north–south axis traced by the Avenue of the Dead, that ends at the magnificent Pirámide de la Luna (Pyramid of the Moon). At the southern end is the vast Citadel, a walled quadrangle with the Temple of Quetzalcóatl against the eastern wall. This astonishing stepped construction (around AD 200), later built over, honours the plumed serpent (Quetzalcóatl) and the rain god (Tláloc) with 366 stone carvings.

Further north looms the gigantic Pirámide del Sol (Pyramid of the Sun) and, in its southern shadow, a dramatically designed and enlightening new museum displaying priceless exhibits and a huge scale model of the site, crossed by a transparent walkway. At the northwest end of the avenue, flanking another large ceremonial area, stands the extensively restored Palacio de Quetzalpapálotl, part of the priests' residential complex. Here, on an

Walk in the shadows of an exceptional civilisation and see fabulous carvings at the Templo de Quetzalcóatl (inset)

elevated patio, are square columns carved with bird and butterfly designs and remnants of red wall friezes. More patios and lower chambers show depictions of the jaguar god, conch shells and birds. A climb to the summit of the Pirámide de la Luna offers a final, sweeping view of this once great city.

10
Xochimilco

🔲 42B1

🚉 Tren Ligero: La Noria, from Tasqueña

🚢 Fixed boat prices at Embarcadero

♿ Few

✋ Moderate

↔ Museo Anáhuacalli (▶ 35)

❓ Two-hour tours available (in Spanish) of Parque Ecológico ☎ (673) 8061/7890 or in English through travel agents

Museo Dolores Olmedo Patiño

✉ Avenida México 5843, La Noria

☎ (555) 1016

🕐 Tue–Sun 10–6 except 25 Dec, 1 Jan and Easter Sun

🍴 Pleasant open-air café (£)

Brilliantly painted punts await the festive Sunday hordes

Xochimilco is a throwback to the capital's Aztec origins, with its canals and 'floating' nursery gardens.

On the far southern edge of Mexico City, weekends are an excuse for feasting on fresh air while cruising the verdant canals of Xochimilco to the strident tunes of *mariachis*. Brilliantly decorated, pole-propelled *trajineras* (Mexican gondolas), packed with large groups or families, combine with countless flower- and food-sellers in canoes to create watery traffic jams. But this is Mexico, and chaos is part of the colourful picture.

The tradition of 'floating' gardens goes back to the Aztecs, who, due to a shortage of farmland, devised a method of creating islands rooted by willow trees. These *chinampas* were used to grow fruit, vegetables and flowers to supply Tenochtitlán, the capital.

Xochimilco covers an area of 135sq km that includes the town itself, with its beautiful 16th-century church of San Bernardino de Siena, beside several others, an archae-ological museum, and the Parque Ecológico, an extensive area of grasslands, lagoons and canals. This is an ideal destination for birdwatchers, families or anyone desperate for unpolluted air close to the city centre.

Xochimilco's final offering is a fascinating private **museum** housed in an atmospheric 400-year-old hacienda. The vast landscaped grounds are an added draw. Named after its owner, Dolores Olmedo, the museum exhibits an important collection of paintings by Diego Rivera and his wives, Frida Kahlo and Angelina Beloff, as well as pre-Hispanic artefacts (some probably copies) and an impressive collection of folk art.

What to See

Above: ponchos for sale
Right: a Chamulan in Chiapas

Tijuana Mexicali
San Luis
Río Colorado
Tecate
Ensenada
Puerto Peñasco
4
El Rosario
San
Felipe
Nogales
Agua Prieta
Ciudad
Juárez
Nuevo
Casas Grandes
Casas
Grandes
Bahía de los Ángeles
Bahía
Kino
Hermosillo
Chihuahua
Pinturas Rupestres
Punta
Eugenia
Guerrero
Negro
Guaymas
Cuauhtémoc
Laguna Ojo
de Liebre
San Ignacio
Santa Rosalía
Ciudad
Obregón
Creel
Barranca
del Cobre
Ciudad
Jiménez
Monclo
Laguna
San Ignacio
Mulegé
El Fuerte
Hidalgo
del Parral
Loreto
Los Mochis
Tepehuanes
Torreón
San Carlos
Bahía Magdalena
Isla
Magdalena
Santiago
Papasquiaro
La Paz
Durango
San José
del Cabo
Culiacán
Cabo
San Lucas
Cabo San Lucas
(Los Cabos)
Mazatlán
Zacatecas
Acaponeta
Aguascalientes
Islas
Marías
Tepic
Leó
Guadalajara
Irapua
Puerto Vallarta
Cabo Corrientes
L. de Chapala
Zamo
Autlán de
Navarro
Colima
Morel
Uruapan
Manzanillo
Presa del
Infiernillo
Ixtap
Zihuatane

Golfo
Baja
California
Sonora
Sierra
Madre
Sierra
Madre
Occidental
Grande o Bravo del Norte
Conchos
Grande de Santiago

0   200   400   600   800 km
0 100 200 300 400 500 miles

A   B   C

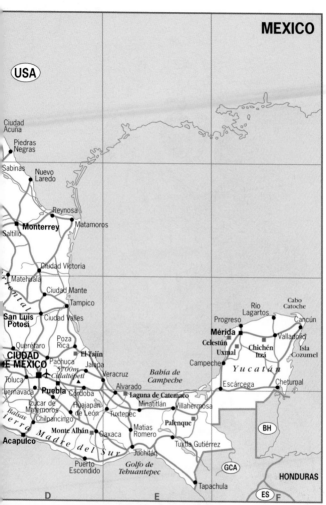

MEXICO

USA

Ciudad Acuña
Piedras Negras
Sabinas
Nuevo Laredo
Reynosa
Monterrey Matamoros
Saltillo
Ciudad Victoria
Matehuala
Ciudad Mante
Tampico
San Luis Potosí Ciudad Valles
Querétaro Poza Rica
CIUDAD E MEXICO Pachuca **El Tajín**
5 700m Citlaltépetl Jalapa
Toluca Veracruz
uernavaca **Puebla** Córdoba
Izúcar de Matemoros Huajapan de León Tuxtepec Minatitlán
Balsas Chilpancingo
Monte Albán Oaxaca Matías Romero
Acapulco
Puerto Escondido Juchitán
Golfo de Tehuantepec
Tapachula

Río Lagartos Cabo Catoche
Progreso Cancún
Mérida Valladolid
Celestún Chichén Isla
Uxmal Itzá Cozumel
Campeche *Yucatán*
Escárcega Cheturnal
Villahermosa
Palenque BH
Tuxtla Gutiérrez
GCA
HONDURAS
ES

Bahía de Campeche
Alvarado
Laguna de Catemaco

Madre del Sur

D E F

Pink flamingos are a familiar sight at Celestún, southwest of Mérida

Central Mexico

Central Mexico is the volcano-studded heart of the nation's colonial heritage. It was the silver mines of Zacatecas and Guanajuato that financed countless cathedrals in Spain, while a stream of baroque masterpieces was created in a roll-call of towns from Cuernavaca to Querétaro, Morelia and Puebla.

For today's conquistadores, this is not only one of the most culturally rewarding regions, where interest ranges from local craft specialities to exceptionally designed museums and dramatic archaeological sites, but it also offers spectacular scenery, lakes, forests and generally cooler temperatures. Political events have marked this region – Morelia was the birthplace of José María Morelos, one of the leaders of the Independence movement, and the state of Morelos was the battleground of Emiliano Zapata, the revolutionary hero.

> *'And when we saw all those cities and villages built in the water, and other great towns on dry land... (it) seemed like an enchanted vision from the tale of Amadis.'*
>
> BERNAL DÍAZ
> *The Conquest of New Spain* (1568)

─────●─────

Papier-mâché skeletons are a common sight during Day of the Dead celebrations

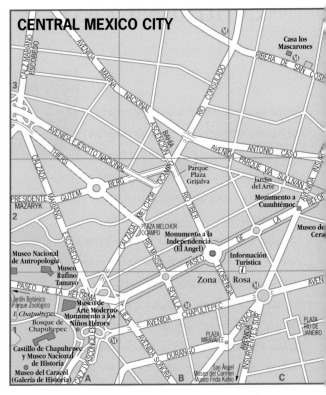

CENTRAL MEXICO CITY

Casa los Mascarones

RIBERA DE SAN COS

Parque Plaza Grijalva

Jardín del Arte

Monumento a Cuauhtémoc

PLAZA MELCHOR OCAMPO Monumento a la Independencia (El Angel)

Museo de Cera

Información Turística

Zona Rosa

Museo Nacional de Antropología

Museo Rufino Tamayo

Jardín Botánico Parque Zoológico L. Chapultepec

Museo de Arte Moderno
Monumento a los Niños Héroes

Bosque de Chapultepec

PLAZA RÍO DE JANEIRO

PLAZA MIRAVALLE

Castillo de Chapultepec y Museo Nacional de Historia

Museo del Caracol (Galería de Historia)

San Angel Museo del Carmen Museo Frida Kahlo

Mexico City

Vibrant, ever-expanding and highly polluted, Mexico City is the political, cultural and economic heart of the country. Rimmed by volcanoes and lying at an altitude of 2,200m, Mexico's capital now claims over 20 million inhabitants. All of them surrender to the precariousness of living in a city that is gradually sinking into the underground Lago de Texcoco, is plagued by crime and yet survived the terrible earthquake of 1985 with incredible civic solidarity. But despite all its negative factors, no one should pass up on a chance to spend a few days in this stimulating megalopolis.

Mexico City (Ciudad de México) can be divided into three main zones of interest: the Centro Histórico and Alameda area; the Zona Rosa and Chapultepec; and, far to the south, San Angel, Coyoacán and Xochimilco. From Aztec

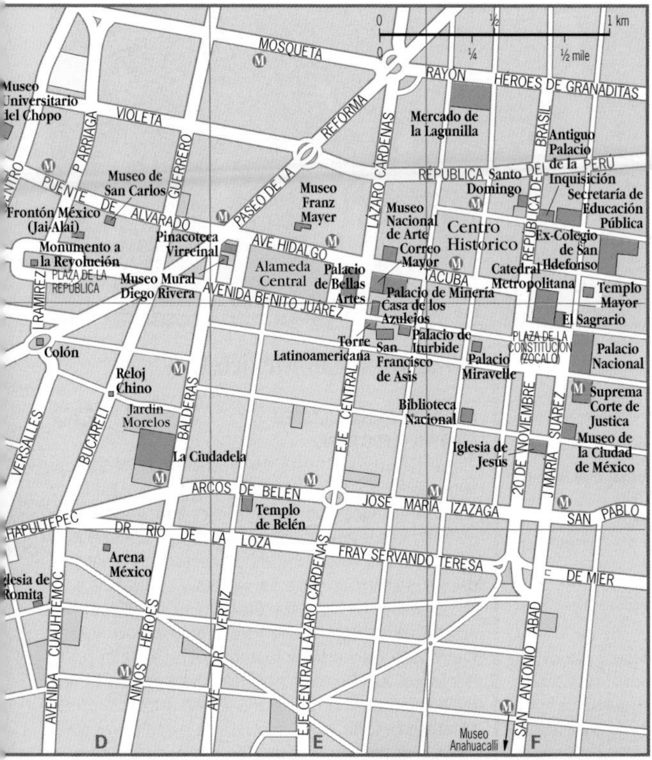
0
½
1 km
0
¼
½ mile
MOSQUETA
RAYÓN
HÉROES DE GRANADITAS
Museo Universitario del Chopo
VIOLETA
P. ARRIAGA
PASEO DE LA REFORMA
LÁZARO CÁRDENAS
Mercado de la Lagunilla
BRASIL
Antiguo Palacio de la Inquisición
PERÚ
REPÚBLICA
Santo Domingo
REPÚBLICA DE
Secretaría de Educación Pública
Museo de San Carlos
GUERRERO
Museo Franz Mayer
PUENTE DE ALVARADO
Frontón México (Jai-Alai)
Pinacoteca Virreinal
Museo Nacional de Arte
Centro Histórico
Ex-Colegio de San Ildefonso
Monumento a la Revolución
AVE HIDALGO
Correo Mayor
PLAZA DE LA REPÚBLICA
Alameda Central
Palacio de Bellas Artes
Catedral Metropolitana
Templo Mayor
Museo Mural Diego Rivera
TACUBA
AVENIDA BENITO JUÁREZ
Palacio de Minería
Casa de los Azulejos
El Sagrario
RAMIREZ
Palacio de Iturbide
PLAZA DE LA CONSTITUCIÓN (ZÓCALO)
Palacio Nacional
Colón
Torre Latinoamericana
San Francisco de Asís
Palacio Miravelle
Reloj Chino
EJE CENTRAL
20 DE NOVIEMBRE
Suprema Corte de Justica
Jardín Morelos
Biblioteca Nacional
SUÁREZ
VERSALLES
BUCARELI
BALDERAS
Museo de la Ciudad de México
La Ciudadela
Iglesia de Jesús
J. MARÍA
ARCOS DE BELÉN
JOSÉ MARÍA IZAZAGA
SAN PABLO
CHAPULTEPEC
Templo de Belén
DR. RÍO DE LA LOZA
FRAY SERVANDO TERESA
DE MIER
Arena México
Iglesia de Romita
CUAUHTÉMOC
NIÑOS HÉROES
DR. VERTIZ
EJE CENTRAL LÁZARO CÁRDENAS
SAN ANTONIO ABAD
AVENIDA
AVE
D
E
F
Museo Anahuacalli

ruins to impressive colonial edifices interspersed with modern blocks and wide boulevards, it presents strong visual contrasts. And between these façades cruises a stream of traffic, monopolised by the ubiquitous Volkswagen 'beetles' – the mainstay of the taxi business. In the Centro Histórico, pedicabs have been introduced, offering an alternative, more leisurely form of transport, while the excellent metro system covers the entire city.

Finding your way round can be tiring and frustrating, but the streets, alive with colour, noise and activity, more than compensate for this.

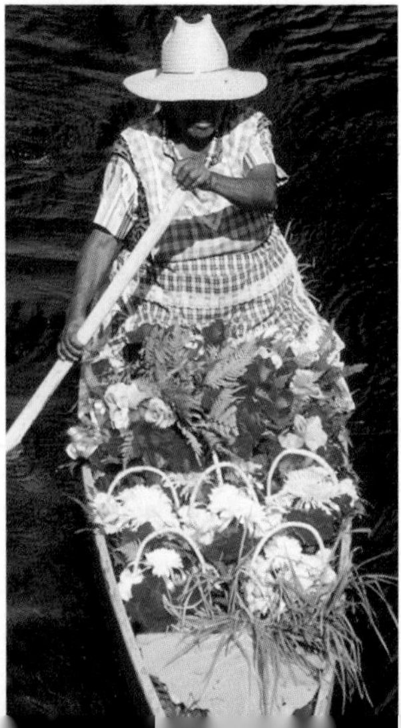

Flowers and food for sale on Xochimilco's waterways

What to See in Mexico City

🗺 32A1

Museo Nacional de Historia
☎ 286 9920
🕐 Tue–Sun 9–5
🍴 Café (£) on premises
Ⓜ Chapultepec
♿ Few
🎫 Cheap; free Sun

*Chapultepec's monument
to the heroic army cadets,
martyred during the
Mexican–American War*

BOSQUE DE CHAPULTEPEC
(CHAPULTEPEC PARK)

This extensive park marks the western limits of the city centre and is a favourite with some half-a-million city dwellers for weekend walks, picnics and spontaneous open-air entertainment. Lakes, woods, lawns, museums, an amusement park, a zoo and restaurants are among its diverse offerings: an entire day can easily be spent here.

Crowning the hill is the Castillo de Chapultepec, an austere construction dating from 1785 that now houses the **Museo Nacional de Historia**. Here, a rather dusty display covers Mexican history, and there are murals and the sumptuous royal apartments of the hapless Emperor Maximilian and his wife, Carlota. Don't miss the sweeping views from the terrace café. The castle is reached by a winding path from the Monumento a los Niños Heroes (Monument to the Young Heroes), at the main park entrance, which passes the snail-like Museo del Caracol (covering Independence and the Revolution) on the way.

The star of Chapultepec is the Museo Nacional de Antropología (► 21), located on the busy Paseo de la Reforma that slices across the park. Near by are two major art museums: the Museo de Arte Moderno, and the Museo Rufino Tamayo (which concentrates on temporary exhibitions of contemporary art). Further west lies the Jardín Botánico, boating lakes and restaurants, a high-tech children's museum, Museo Papalote (► 110), an amusement park, and the zoo that claims to be the world's oldest, as it existed during Aztec rule.

CATEDRAL METROPOLITANA
(METROPOLITAN CATHEDRAL)

Dominating the Zócalo, Mexico City's main historic square, is this massive cathedral (Latin America's largest), which was begun in 1563, although its baroque façade dates from 1681 and the asymmetrical towers and dome were

🗺 33F3
✉ Zócalo, Centro Histórico
🕐 Daily 8–8
🍴 Cafés (£) on main square
Ⓜ Zócalo ♿ Good
🎫 Free

added in 1813. The walls incorporate stones from the ruins of the Aztec Temple of Quetzalcóatl, but far more visible is the gilded baroque of the Capilla de Los Reyes (Chapel of the Kings) that glows in the gloomy interior. Subsidence is an ongoing problem – note the slope from high altar to the entrance – and metal structural supports are unfortunately highly visible. Next door stands the Churrigueresque-style El Sagrario (The Sacred), currently closed, with a remarkably ornate façade dating from 1760.

The Catedral Metropolitana, built over a period of 250 years, looms over the historic heart of the city

MUSEO ANÁHUACALLI (HOUSE OF ANÁHUAC)   ✪✪✪

This outstanding museum is unfortunately located on the far southern edge of Coyoacán and requires some effort to visit. Conceived by the famous muralist and artist Diego Rivera, it embodies his identification with Mesoamerican culture. The pyramidal lava-stone structure houses his collection of 60,000 pre-Hispanic artefacts and a studio where he worked briefly before his death in 1957, leaving some unfinished paintings. Dark, labyrinthine corridors with onyx windows, stone ceiling mosaics, open terraces, arches and stepped, altar-like displays all echo pre-Hispanic forms.

➕ 33F1
✉ Calle del Museo 150, San Pablo de Tepetlapa
☎ 677 2984
🕐 Tue–Sun 10–2, 3–6. Closed Holy Week
Ⓜ Taxqueña, then taxi
♿ None
💰 Moderate; free Sun

Brightly decorated mask on show in the Museo Anáhuacalli

35

A Walk through San Angel

A wander through the relaxed neighbourhood of San Angel, along tree-lined cobbled streets, takes in ancient churches, museums and shops.

From the pesero bus terminal walk up Avenida Revolución to the Museo del Carmen (► opposite) on your right. After visiting this monument, cross the avenue to the Centro Cultural and walk along Calle Madero to Plaza San Jacinto, lined with shops and restaurants.

On the right-hand side, the 18th-century Casa del Risco offers an unusual ceramic and shell-encrusted fountain, while inside it displays 16th- to 18th-century Mexican and European art. Next door is the Bazar del Sábado, a large crafts market open only on Saturdays. On the far corner of the plaza stands the beautiful 16th-century church and former monastery of San Jacinto.

Continue along this street, past the crossroads, when it becomes Calle Miguel Hidalgo. At the 17th-century Casa Blanca turn right into Licenciados, following it downhill into Calle Leandro Valle.

These quiet streets offer a classic vision of Mexico City's wealthier residences, often brightly painted and set behind high walls, in a wide range of architectural styles.

At the main crossroads cross Altavista, passing a beautiful 18th-century hacienda on your left (now the San Angel Inn). Opposite stands the Museo Estudio Diego Rivera.

This blue structure was designed in 1930 for Rivera and includes a smaller, adjoining structure intended for Frida Kahlo. Rivera's studio, where he died in 1957, gives a fascinating insight into his last years.

Walk east down Altavista to Avenida Revolución and the Museo de Arte Carrillo Gil opposite, before returning south to the bus terminal.

The attractive church of San Jacinto stands in a peaceful walled garden

Distance
About 3km

Time
2–3 hours, depending on stops

Start/end point
San Angel bus terminal
 32C1

Lunch
San Angel Inn (£££)
🞖 32C1
✉ Calle Diego Rivera 50
☎ 616 1402 (booking essential)

MUSEO DEL CARMEN (CARMEN MUSEUM) ●●

On the edge of the delightful residential area of San Angel, in a cloistered garden, is this former Carmelite monastery, built in 1617 with tiled domes. The attractive, unusual interior encompasses floral friezes, wood and gesso ceiling reliefs, tiles and frescoes. Displayed throughout the former chapels and cells is an important collection of baroque religious art and, in the crypt, a somewhat ghoulish line-up of mummies.

- 32C1
- ✉ Avenida Revolución 4, corner Calle Monasterio, San Angel
- ☎ 550 4896
- 🕐 Tue–Sun 10–5
- 🍴 Cafés/restaurants (£–££) on Plaza San Jacinto
- 🚌 San Angel *pesero* bus down Insurgentes
- ♿ Moderate

MUSEO FRANZ MAYER (FRANZ MAYER MUSEUM) ●●●

Opened in 1986 in a superbly restored 16th-century mansion, this museum contains an exceptional collection of 16th- to 19th-century fine and applied arts, amassed by German immigrant and construction magnate, Franz Mayer. Influences and contrasts are highlighted between Asian, Arab, European and Mexican styles, and priceless exhibits include paintings by Velázquez, Rivera and Zubarán. Inlaid furniture, tapestries, silver and gold objects, wooden sculptures, glass and ceramics complete this impressive collection.

- 33E3
- ✉ Avenida Hidalgo 45, Colonia Guerrero
- ☎ 518 2265/71
- 🕐 Tue–Sun 10–5
- 🍴 Excellent Café del Claustro (£)
- 🚇 Hidalgo, Bellas Artes
- ♿ Good
- ♿ Moderate

MUSEO FRIDA KAHLO (FRIDA KAHLO MUSEUM) ●●●

Deep indigo and red-ochre walls picked out with brilliant green window-frames announce the eclectic and flamboyant tastes of Mexico's foremost woman artist, Frida Kahlo. Located in the pretty tree-lined streets of Coyoacán, where she spent most of her life, her family home reflects her wide-ranging interests and obsessions, and includes some poignant items such as the wheelchair to which she was confined in her last years, her four-poster bed and her last, unfinished painting (a portrait of Stalin). Beside these is a wealth of memorabilia in which Kahlo's husband, Diego Rivera, figures strongly, alongside her collections of masks, Teotihuacán sculptures, ex-votos, glass, lacquerware and ceramics.

- 32C1
- ✉ Calle Londres 247, Coyoacán
- ☎ 554 5999
- 🕐 Tue–Sun 10–6
- 🍴 Cafés, restaurants (£–££) on Jardín Centenario
- 🚌 General Anaya, then taxi
- ♿ Few
- ♿ Moderate

A 1930s self-portrait by Frida Kahlo, aged 23, prefigures her increasingly morbid later works

MUSEO NACIONAL DE ANTROPOLOGÍA (► 21, TOP TEN)

PALACIO DE BELLAS ARTES

Sidebar 1

🕂 33E3

✉ Corner Avenida Juárez and Eje Central, Centro

☎ 510 1388/512 2593

🕐 Palace: daily 10–6; museum: Tue–Sun 10–6

🍴 Café del Palacio (££)

Ⓜ Bellas Artes

♿ Very good, except front steps

🎫 Free

❓ Ballet Folklórico: Wed, Sun mornings and Sun evenings

Sidebar 2

🕂 33F2

✉ Zócalo

🕐 Daily 9–5

🍴 Cafés (£) on Zócalo

Ⓜ Zócalo

♿ Good

🎫 Free, but bring identification

🔀 Catedral Metropolitana (► 34), Templo Mayor (► opposite)

❓ Military lowering of flag daily before sunset with brass band

The ornate Bellas Artes combines architectural styles from 1900 to 1934

PALACIO DE BELLAS ARTES (PALACE OF FINE ARTS)   ✪✪✪

Another of Mexico City's architectural showstoppers presides over the lively park, Alameda Central, on the western edge of the Centro Histórico. The Bellas Artes is a popular cultural centre, with excellent temporary exhibitions, a theatre where the renowned Ballet Folklórico performs, a large bookshop, gift shop, restaurant and a display of murals by the 'big three' – Rivera, Orozco and Siqueiros – alongside Tamayo, on the upper floors. Set around a vast marble-lined atrium, the interior is pure art deco, in total contrast to the exuberant domed and colonnaded exterior.

PALACIO NACIONAL (NATIONAL PALACE)   ✪✪

Mexico's first parliament is housed within this vast edifice flanking the eastern side of the Zócalo. The 17th-century palace replaced two previous ones, and is still the political powerhouse of Mexico as it holds the offices of the President, the National Archives and the Federal Treasury. Above the main entrance hangs the highly symbolic 'Freedom Bell' that rang out in the town of Dolores, on 15 September 1810 to announce the fight for Independence. This is rung annually on the eve of Independence Day by the President to teeming masses gathered in the square.

Inside the courtyard a grand staircase leads up past extensive murals by Rivera: a *tour de force* that covers the history of Mexico. It is well worth following a guide to have the endless details explained. A small musem on the second floor, dedicated to Mexico's most revered president, Benito Juárez, is being renovated.

TEMPLO MAYOR (GREAT TEMPLE) ✪✪✪

On the northeastern corner of the Zócalo is one of the few Aztec sites that remain. When it was completed in 1487, the temple consisted of seven superimposed structures, each one involving a four-day dedication ceremony and several thousand sacrificial victims. It was unearthed by accident in 1978 during construction of the metro. Four years of excavations uncovered hundreds of superb sculptures, now housed in an impressive modern museum behind the site, designed to resemble the temple layout.

Visitors can wander through the temple ruins on raised walkways that give close-ups on the altars devoted to Tláloc, the god of rain, and Huitzilopochtli, the fearsome god of war, along with replicas of sculptures. Highly visible is the wall of skulls standing in front of the museum, while inside, one of the most outstanding exhibits is a huge carved stone disc depicting the dismembered goddess of the moon, Coyolxauhqui.

TORRE LATINOAMERICANA ✪
(LATIN-AMERICAN TOWER)

This lofty downtown landmark was the capital's first skyscraper when completed in 1956, but has since been surpassed by others. Towering 139m, it survived the 1985 earthquake and other tremors due to ingenious anti-seismic foundations that incorporate 361 concrete stilts. Today, it offers the best vantage point for views over the city (on rare, smogless days), particularly breathtaking at night. On the 44th floor is an outdoor viewing deck.

XOCHIMILCO (► 26, TOP TEN)

✚ 33F3
⊠ Seminario 8, Centro
☎ 542 4787/0606
🕐 Tue–Sun 9–5
🍽 Cafés and restaurants
   (£–££) in and near Zócalo
Ⓜ Zócalo
♿ Very good in museum,
   not on site
💵 Cheap; free Sun
🔁 Palacio Nacional
   (► opposite), Catedral
   Metropolitana (► 34)

A serpent's head – one of many Aztec sculptures unearthed at the Templo Mayor

✚ 33E2
⊠ Corner Avenida Madero
   and Lázaro Cárdenas
🕐 Daily, 9:30AM–10:30PM
🍽 Cafés and restaurants
   (£–££) in Centro Histórico
Ⓜ Bellas Artes, San Juan de
   Letrán
💵 Moderate

Food & Drink

Mexican cuisine combines traditional indigenous recipes and ingredients with Spanish and North American influences. As varied as the country's scenery, the food of Mexico covers every budget, from street-corner *tacos* to sophisticated dishes that are reverting to pre-Hispanic recipes after decades of 'international' cuisine.

Flipping fresh tortillas at a roadside stall to provide the Mexican staple diet

National Snacks

Corn *tortillas* have been the staff of life for centuries, and still accompany most dishes, while *tacos* and *burritos* are stuffed versions that make filling snacks. Less flavoursome wheat *tortillas* are now making inroads in the north, while dark-blue or red versions are made from special types of corn. The ubiquitous *tacos*, sold on every street of the country, are crisp fried *tortillas* stuffed with a fantastic variety of fillings and often topped with grated cheese. If you are careful about where you buy them, *tacos* make delicious and very cheap appetisers. In the south, *tamales* enter the field. These are similar, except that the ingredients are wrapped and steamed in corn husks or banana leaves and may sometimes be sweet. Further variations on the *tortilla* theme include *enchiladas* (cheese or chicken *tacos* baked in a spicy sauce) and *quesadillas*, mainly cheese-filled *tortillas*. A common accompaniment to the above is *frijoles*, red beans in a mushy sauce.

Timing

To get the most out of Mexican cuisine, follow the Mexican's rhythm. This entails large breakfasts that include fresh fruit and eggs – try *huevos rancheros*, fried eggs and diced chilli in a tomato sauce atop a *tortilla*. Mexican coffee, apart from in the coffee-growing region of Veracruz, is generally a diluted affair, so real *aficionados* should order espresso, Italian-style coffee available in most up-market restaurants. Tea is also a pale imitation of the real thing, but Mexicans make up for this with a fantastic selection of fresh fruit juices (*jugos de*

frutas), and you can order your own combination.

The main meal in Mexico is lunch, eaten at any time between 2 and 5PM, when restaurants offer good-value set menus (*comidas corridas*). Dinner, if taken at all, is generally after 9PM. Tourists who may not want a large lunch will find that resorts cater for European eating hours, but if you travel off the beaten track you will only find up-market restaurants open in the evenings.

Essential ingredients for the ritual of tequila drinking: squeezed lime, salt and the elixir itself

Guacamole may have travelled the world, but its original Mexican version is unbeatable

Seafood

Mexican seafood is obviously best along the coast, and resorts cook up exceptionally fresh fish such as *huachinango* (red snapper), *robalo* (snook) and prawn dishes (*camarones*). However, be warned, *sopa de camarón* is one of Mexico's spiciest dishes. Freshwater fish includes *pescado blanco*, a delicate white fish from Lago de Pátzcuaro, and *langostino*, a large crayfish usually cooked *al mojo de ajo*. This popular seafood preparation consists of fried garlic: again, be warned!

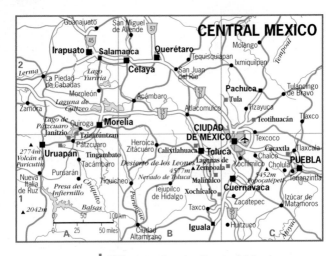

What to See in Central Mexico

CHOLULA ⊙

Once a major ceremonial town dedicated to Quetzalcóatl, Cholula suffered extensive destruction by Cortés' army on its march to Mexico City. Numerous shrines and churches include the Convento Franciscano (1549) and the 18th-century Capilla Real with its 49 domes. The **Gran Pirámide**, the largest pyramid in the Americas, dominates this otherwise nondescript town. Crowning the summit is the 16th-century Templo de Nuestra Señora de los Remedios (Temple of Our Lady of Remedies), while below, some 8km of tunnels have revealed extensive remains of murals. A small museum near the tunnel entrance houses copies of the frescoes.

CUERNAVACA ⊙⊙

Often dubbed the 'city of eternal spring', Cuernavaca is a favourite bolt-hole for the capital's wealthier inhabitants. Despite a population of over one million, and the largest number of swimming pools per capita in the world, it has a delightful centre, and, situated only 65km south of Mexico City, makes an attractive alternative base. Two adjoining plazas form the heart of town, over which looms the **Palacio de Cortés** (1530), a massive fortress-palace housing a fascinating museum of regional archaeology, colonial history and the Revolution. There is also a masterful mural by Diego Rivera depicting Spanish oppression of the indigenous peoples.

In front lie the plazas, focal points for a crafts market, promenading and general festivities. A short walk west up Calle Hidalgo brings you to the magnificent Catedral (1530), built by the Franciscans. Despite being one of

Sidebar (left column)

✚ 42C1
ℹ Opposite main entrance
⬌ Puebla (► 48)
❓ Guides available to explore main tunnel

Gran Pirámide

✉ Highway 190, Cholula
🕐 Daily 9–6
🍴 Restaurant Choloyán (£), Avenida Morelos
♿ Few
💳 Moderate; free Sun

✚ 42C1
ℹ Avenida Morelos Sur 187, Colonia La Palma ☎ 143709

Palacio de Cortés

✉ Avenida Benito Juárez
☎ (73) 128171/126996
🕐 Tue–Sun 10–5
🍴 Restaurants and cafés (£–££) on the zócalo
♿ Good (ground floor only)
💳 Moderate

Mexico's oldest churches, its interior is strikingly modern. Across Avenida Morelos is the Jardín Borda, a beautiful landscaped garden surrounding a mansion (1783) built by French silver magnate José de la Borda. It was once a favourite retreat for Emperor Maximilian. Historical documents, folk art and temporary art shows are among the exhibits.

GUADALAJARA ✪✪

Mexico's second-largest city offers a compact historical centre, a pleasant climate and lively traditions from *mariachis* to glass-blowing. The monuments are dotted around four central plazas surrounding the Catedral, a massive edifice that combines numerous architectural styles due to repeated reconstruction. Flanking the Plaza de Armas outside is the Palacio Nacional, where Miguel Hidalgo declared an end to slavery, an event captured by Orozco's powerful murals on its walls.

Immediately north is the fascinating **Museo Regional de Jalisco** (1701) housed in a former seminary. Exhibits cover pre-Hispanic artefacts, religious and colonial paintings, decorative arts and handicrafts by Jalisco's Huichol and Cora Indians. To the east stands the neo-classical Teatro Delgollado, where Guadalajara's state orchestra and Grupo Folklórico perform. From here, the Plaza Tapatía stretches east to the impressive Instituto Cultural Cabañas, which was designed as an orphanage in 1805. This is now the focal point for the city's cultural activities, as well as housing a homage to José Clemente Orozco, the city's renowned 20th-century painter, whose vigorous murals adorn the domed chapel.

Other offerings include a labyrinthine crafts and food market, the Mercado Libertad, and, near by, the Plaza de los Mariachis, where cafés and restaurants are invaded by *mariachis* daily.

Not to be missed are the villages of Tlaquepaque and Tonalá, now engulfed by the urban sprawl. Tlaquepaque makes a colourful outing by bus from the centre. Elegant 19th-century mansions converted into restaurants and crafts boutiques radiate from the Jardín Hidalgo and El Parián. The latter is a remodelled structure housing more crafts shops and restaurants. A few kilometres further on lies Tonalá, with its glass and pottery workshops.

➕ 28C2
ℹ️ Plaza Tapatía, Morelos 102 ☎ 614 0123
🚆 Laguna de Chapala (► 44)

Museo Regional de Jalisco

✉️ Corner Avenida Hidalgo and Liceo
☎ (3) 614 2227
🕐 Tue–Sat 9–7, Sun 9–1:45
🍴 Cafés and restaurants (£) on plazas
♿ Few
💵 Moderate

The Palacio de Gobierno (1643) on Guadalajara's Plaza de Armas, one of the four squares surrounding the Catedral

Olmec heads at Jalapa

🗺 29D2
🚌 Avenida Avila Camacho
191 ☎ (28)
187402/187424
🔄 El Tajín (▶ 43)

Museo de Antropología
✉ Avenida Xalapa, Estado
de Veracruz
☎ (28) 150708/150920
🕐 Mon–Fri 9–6, Sat–Sun
9–5
🍴 Cafeteria (£) in museum
♿ Excellent
💰 Moderate

🗺 28C2
✉ 50km southeast of
Guadalajara, 40 minutes
by car
🍴 Vast choice of cafés and
restaurants (£–£££) along
northwest shore
ℹ Tourist office in
Guadalajara (▶ 43)
♿ Good

GUANAJUATO (▶ 18, TOP TEN)

JALAPA   ✪✪

Blazing sun in the morning and cooler mists in the afternoon characterise Jalapa's picturesque location, high in the coffee-growing hills inland from Veracruz. On the horizon is the Cofre de Perote volcano (4,282m) overlooking this lively university town, with its atmospheric colonial heart of steep, winding streets, gardens, parks and grandiose administrative buildings. The star sight is the excellent **Museo de Antropología**, an imaginatively designed modern building at the northern end of town. Here sunlit patios and terraced marble halls opening on to a landscaped park display a collection of the pre-Hispanic cultures of the Gulf region. Giant basalt heads from the Olmec centre of San Lorenzo vie with the wonderful 'smiling' sculptures of the Totonacs at El Tajín and the superb pottery of the northern Huastecs.

LAGUNA DE CHAPALA   ✪

The warm climate of Mexico's largest natural lake has long attracted a stream of expatriates, from writers such as D H Lawrence and Sybille Bedford to today's 6,000 North American retirees. Sleepy fishing villages stud the lake shore, but the main animation is along the northwest shore at Chapala, Ajijic and Jocotepec. Boats trips visit the two islands of Los Alacranes and Mexcala, the former boasting the lake's most scenic fish restaurants. More authentic in style, and the source of colourful handwoven *serapes* (shawls), is Jocotepec.

MORELIA ✪✪

The uncontested architectural jewel of fertile Michoacán is its capital, Morelia, a dynamic yet compact university town. Although founded in 1541 as Valladolid, it was renamed Morelia at independence to honour Jose María Morelos, a native son and key figure in the movement. Dominating the central plaza is a massive pink-stone cathedral, said to be the third largest in the Americas. Harmonious arcades, churches, colleges and imposing colonial buildings radiate from here and include the magnificent mansion that now houses the **Museo Regional Michoacán**, covering local ethnography, archaeology and colonial history. One block north is Mexico's oldest university, the Colegio de San Nicolás, and a few steps further the superbly proportioned Palacio Clavijero.

42A2
ℹ Palacio Clavijero, Nigromante 79 ☎ (43) 125244
↔ Pátzcuaro (➤ below)

Museo Regional Michoacán
✉ Allende 305, corner of Abasolo
☎ (43) 20407
🕐 Tue–Sat 9–7. Closed 25 Dec, 1 Jan, Easter Sun
🍴 Cafés and restaurants (£) on square
♿ Good
✋ Moderate

PÁTZCUARO ✪✪✪

Situated beside a tranquil lake, Pátzcuaro is an unusual and delightful little town. Quaint cobbled streets lined with neat whitewashed houses wind uphill from Plaza Vasco de Quiroga and Plaza Gertrudis Bocanegra to reach the Basílica de Nuestra Señora de la Salud. Founded in 1554 but rebuilt in 1883, the church contains a much revered corn-paste statue of the Virgin of Health, and on the eighth day of every month pilgrims flock here with requests. Close by is the **Museo de Artes Populares**, housed in a former college dating from 1540. Inside are displayed Michoacán's rich local crafts, from lacquerware to copper. Downhill from Plaza Gertrudis Bocanegra is the lake. From the main *embarcadero*, boats ferry visitors to the commercialised island of Janitzio. Crowning its hilltop is a gigantic statue of Morelos.

42A1
ℹ Plaza Vasco de Quiroga 50, Guion A ☎ (434) 21214
↔ Morelia (➤ above)

Museo de Artes Populares
✉ Enseñanza y Alcantarilla
☎ (434) 21029
🕐 Tue–Sun 9–6
🍴 Cafés and restaurants (£) on main plazas
♿ Good
✋ Cheap

Morelos dominates the island of Janitzio

The dazzling Churrigueresque stucco work in Puebla's Capilla del Rosario took 40 years to complete

🚼 42C1

ℹ️ Avenida 5 Oriente (southern side of Catedral)

Museo Amparo

✉️ Calle 2 Sur, corner Avenida 9 Oriente

☎️ (22) 464646

🕐 Wed–Mon 10–5:30

🍴 Cafés and restaurants (£) on zócalo

♿ Few

🏛️ Moderate

PUEBLA ✪✪

Ringed by four volcanoes and less than two hours by road from the capital is Puebla, Mexico's fourth-largest city. Though very industrialised, it is surprisingly easy-going, and offers fabulous examples of baroque architecture, in particular the Templo de Santo Domingo. At the heart of this church is the Capilla del Rosario (1690), the most sumptuous Dominican construction in the world, where gilded and carved stucco blankets the dome and walls as a backdrop to a bejewelled figure of the Virgin.

The 17th-century Ex-Convento de Santa Rosa, now converted into the Museo de las Artesanías, houses the nuns' kitchens where it is said the famed Pueblan *mole* sauce was invented (► 93). Religious art is exhibited at the Ex-Convento de Santa Monica, full of disguised doorways and secret passageways, dating from 1857 when President Juárez closed all religious structures.

Flanking the south of the zócalo is the vast Catedral, a mixture of various styles due to its prolonged construction between 1575 and 1649. Three blocks southeast is the impressively designed **Museo Amparo**, successfully incorporating high-tech displays of archaeology and viceregal art into a converted 16th-century hospital. Puebla is noted for the Talavera tiles that adorn many façades or domes. Particularly exceptional is the Casa de Alfeñique, home to the Museo Regional, while at Uriarte (► 106) workshops still make this renowned decorative ceramic.

A Drive around Lake Pátzcuaro

Head out of Pátzcuaro on the road to the lake, then follow Highway 14 to Tzintzuntzán, about 20km away.

Above the town is Las Yacatas, a row of stepped, circular pyramids offering sweeping lake views and a small museum. In Tzintzuntzán itself stands the partly ruined 16th-century Templo de San Francisco. Close by are numerous craft outlets for local pottery, woodcarving and straw figures.

Continue to Quiroga, the largest commercial town on the lake. Turn left at the main square and drive a few kilometres to Santa Fe de la Laguna.

Las Yacatas, in Tzintzuntzán, were dedicated to Curicaveri, the Purepecha god of fire

It was here in the 1540s that Don Vasco de Quiroga, Michoacán's first bishop, attempted to set up a model community based on Thomas More's *Utopia*. The 16th-century hospital and chapel still stand and the village square has been completely renovated, together offering an unusual stop.

Continue to skirt the lake through pine forests to the promontory of Chupicaro.

Next stop is San Jerónimo, a sprawling lakeside village jutting out on a small promontory, where activities concentrate on woodcarving and boatbuilding.

Drive on about 15km to the neighbouring villages of Puacuaro, Napizaro and Erongaricuaro, a couple of kilometres apart.

The pure Purepecha inhabitants of Puacuaro and Napizaro specialise in basket-making. In Erongaricuaro (meaning 'look-out tower on the lake') visit the 16th-century Franciscan church and seminary. Handicrafts made here include inlaid furniture, weaving and embroidery.

The road continues around the lake through San Francisco Uricho, Arocutín, Tocuaro and San Pedro, before rejoining Highway 14 and returning to Pátzcuaro.

Distance
About 65km

Time
Allow a leisurely day to include stops

Start/end point
Pátzcuaro
✚ 42A1

Lunch
Restaurants (£) at Chupicaro

QUERÉTARO

The prosperous, industrial town of Querétaro has a harder edge than its neighbours, yet despite this it is rich in history, with a wealth of baroque architecture and a monumental aqueduct (1735). From the central church of San Francisco, a well-designed pedestrianised area, dense with street stalls, leads uphill to the shady, porticoed Plaza de las Armas. This focal point for restaurants and shoe-shiners is the site of the 18th-century Government Palace, situated beside several imposing mansions.

Adjoining San Francisco in another former convent is the fabulous Museo Regional, with its renowned collection of viceregal paintings. Southwest from here are Querétaro's two baroque jewels: the Templo de Santa Clara (1633), with walls covered in high-relief altarpieces, and the equally magnificent Templo de Santa Rosa (1752).

East of San Francisco stands the church and former **Convento de Santa Cruz** (1654) that served as a prison to Emperor Maximilian before his execution in 1867.

SAN MIGUEL DE ALLENDE

This is central Mexico's 'gringo' city, a small, picturesque town buzzing with US expatriates, students and visitors. Reflecting this influx is a plethora of cafés, bars, restaurants and shops geared to their needs. Rising above lively Plaza Allende are the lofty, neo-gothic spires of the Parroquía (1880), while across a side street stands the 18th-century birthplace of Ignacio Allende, an Independence protagonist. Now the **Museo Histórico**, it illustrates the city's history and archaeology alongside contemporary art. Another impressive 18th-century mansion is the Casa del Mayorazgo, its restored interior now houses an art collection. This artistic theme continues in exhibitions at the Centro Cultural Ignacio Ramírez.

42B2

Pasteur Norte 4 ☎ (42) 121412

Convento de Santa Cruz

✉ Avenida Independencia, corner Manuel Acuña

☎ (42) 120235

🕐 Mon–Fri 9–2, 4–6, Sat–Sun 11–6

🍴 Cafés and restaurants (£–££) on Plaza de las Armas

♿ Few

✋ Donation. Guided tours

42B2

Plaza Allende ☎ (415) 26565

Guanajuato (▶ 18)

Museo Histórico

✉ Cuna de Allende 1

🕐 Tue–Sun 10–4. Closed 25 Dec, 1 Jan, Easter Sun

🍴 Cafés and restaurants (£–££) on plaza and near by

♿ Few

✋ Cheap

The fluted spires of the Parroquía soar above San Miguel, now designated a national monument

EL TAJÍN ✪✪✪

Set in lush, scenic hills are the magnificent ruins of the Totonac civilisation (4th–12th centuries). The nearest base is 12km away at Papantla, a pretty little town known for its vanilla plantations. El Tajín's main sight is the Pirámide de los Nichos (Pyramid of the Niches), a striking, tiered edifice incorporating 365 niches rising beside numerous other buildings and at least 10 ball courts. Here, opposing teams played out their ritual game, which ended in sacrifice. The main ball-court walls are carved with fine bas-reliefs depicting players, sacrifices and *pulque*-drinking. Uphill lies El Tajín Chico, where more structures surround the Edificio de las Columnas, decorated with intricate stone mosaics. At the entrance, outside the excellent modern museum, a 30m pole is used by local *voladores* (flying dancers) to re-enact a dangerous but spectacular Totonac ritual.

TAXCO (▶ 23, TOP TEN)

TEOTIHUACÁN (▶ 24–5, TOP TEN)

➕ 29D2
✉ Highway 130, Estado de Veracruz (25km southeast of Poza Rica)
☎ (29) 349981
🕐 Daily 9–5
🍴 Café (£) on site
✋ Moderate; free Sun
❓ *Voladores* perform at noon daily

Above: *Totonac voladores at El Tajín*
Right: *people-watching*

The North &
Baja California

Northern Mexico is the land of interminable
desert rising abruptly into the Sierra Tarahumara
and its canyons (▶ 16), while the coastlines are
washed by the Pacific Ocean, the Mar de Cortés and, to the
east, the Gulf of Mexico. Proximity to the US has generated a
string of unattractive industrialised border cities, but in the long
finger of land known as Baja California lies a tempting variety of
landscapes, from scenic sierra to spectacular, often deserted
beaches. From its border town Tijuana to the southern cape is
a distance of 1,200km, but it is the southern half that offers
most diversity. This is where whale-watching, birdwatching,
sport fishing, scuba diving, riding and trekking take over,
backed up by still-fledgling coastal resorts that contrast with
remote Jesuit missions in the sierra.

*' It is known that to the
right of the Indies there
exists an island called
California very near the
terrestrial paradise. '*

GARCÍA DE MONTALVO
The Adventures of Esplandian
(1510)

───────●───────

A roadside shrine near La Paz echoes the form of the surrounding cacti

What to See in the North and Baja California

BAHÍA DE LOS ANGELES

28A4

Museo de Historia Natural
🍴 Restaurants (£) near by
👍 Good
💵 Cheap

This starkly beautiful bay on the Mar de Cortés makes a welcome change from the dry inland desert and is easily reached from the main highway, 68km away. Facilities include an airstrip, several good hotels, trailer parks, restaurants and the **Museo de Historia Natural**. On the horizon lies Isla Angel de la Guarda, a large island reserve, while the waters of the bay are alive with dolphins, finback whales and sea lions. Boat trips can easily be arranged.

BARRANCA DEL COBRE (► 16, TOP TEN)

LOS CABOS

28B2
ℹ️ Edificio Fonatur, Muelle Turístico, Cabo San Lucas
☎ (114) 32540

Centro Cultural de Los Cabos
✉️ Behind Presidente Forum Resort
☎ (114) 21504
🕐 Tue–Sun 9–5, Wed 9–1
🍴 Cafés and restaurants (££) on Paseo Mijáres
👍 Good
💵 Cheap

At the tip of Baja lie the twin resorts of Cabo San Lucas and San José del Cabo, 30 minutes apart but with quite distinct atmospheres. Cabo San Lucas is a boisterous, half-finished modern resort while San José retains a quaint Mexican village atmosphere beneath its touristic veneer. Los Cabos offer luxury hotels, golf courses, sport fishing, surfing, scuba diving at the unique underwater sand cascades, whale-watching and horse riding in the sierra.

San José dates back to 1730 when its Jesuit mission was founded. Adjacent Paseo Mijáres, with its stone and stucco 19th-century houses, is now the focal point for restaurants, bars, shops and real-estate agents. At the river estuary, a small **cultural centre** displays arts and crafts, fossils and reproduction cave-paintings, while next to this is an ecological reserve, home to 200 bird species.

The Baja peninsula ends at El Arco, a massive rock arch that terminates the headland. Boat trips from the marina visit this landmark and El Faro Viejo (Old Lighthouse), which offers panoramic views. Pelicans, seals, sea lions, dolphins and whales can be seen, while underwater is a paradise for snorkellers and divers.

A heavily laden beach vendor at Cabo San Lucas

CASAS GRANDES

28B4
✉️ Zona Arqueológica de Paquimé, Casas Grandes
☎ (169) 24140
🕐 Tue–Sun 10–5
🍴 Cafeteria (£)
💵 Cheap; free Sun

This is the most important archaeological site in northern Mexico, best reached from Ciudad Juárez. Thought to date from AD 1000, Casas Grandes was abandoned in the mid-14th century following attacks by Apaches. Structures on site include platforms, ball courts, underground chambers and the remains of three-storey adobe houses. Excavations have unearthed rich finds of Paquimé pottery, necklaces of semi-precious stones and carvings of Quetzalcóatl, some displayed in the museum.

+ 28C4

i Libertad 1300, 1st floor,
  Edificio Agustín Melgar
  ☎ (14) 293300

Museo de la Revolución
✉ Calle Décima 3014
☎ (14) 162958
🕐 Tue–Sun 10–5
🍴 None
♿ None
💵 Cheap

*Chihuahua's cathedral
was begun in 1726 but
only completed in 1826*

CHIHUAHUA ✪

Capital of Mexico's largest state, Chihuahua means 'dry,
sandy place' in Náhuatl, yet today this region prospers
from cattle ranches, silver, gold and copper mines and
apple orchards. The city is the eastern terminus for the
Chihuahua–Pacífico railway (➤ 16), but also offers a
number of sights, some linked to Chihuahua's role in the
War of Independence and the Revolution. On the central
zócalo stands the baroque Catedral, and two blocks east is
the Palacio Federal, where Miguel Hidalgo was imprisoned
in 1811 before his execution. Opposite stands the pink
Palacio del Gobierno, originally a Jesuit college, with
murals depicting Chihuahua's history.

South of the centre are two major museums. The
Museo Regional is housed in the Quinta Gameros, a
lavishly decorated mansion displaying art nouveau kitsch
and a display of Paquimé pottery from Casas Grandes.
Four blocks south is the **Museo de la Revolución**, in the
mansion where revolutionary leader Pancho Villa lived.
Exhibits include photographs, arms, documents and the
black 1922 Dodge peppered with bullet holes in which Villa
was assassinated.

+ 28A4

i Tourist and Convention
  Bureau, Lázaro Cárdenas,
  corner Miramar

Bodegas Santo Tomás
✉ Avenida Miramar 666
☎ (617) 82509
🕐 Daily tours at 11, 1, 3
♿ Few
💵 Moderate

ENSENADA ✪

Just over 100km south of Tijuana lies Ensenada, Baja
California's most popular resort, receiving half a million
visitors each year. These are mostly Californians on
weekend drinking, eating, shopping and sport fishing
sprees, but during the week the town and its bay return to
more tranquil fishing and shipping activities. Ultra-fresh
seafood is available at the Mercado de Pescas opposite
the pier, and local wine can be sampled at the wineries:
the largest, **Bodegas Santo Tomás**, offers daily wine
tastings in its converted warehouse.

South of town is La Bufadora, a blowhole where wave

Historic national heroes are honoured in Ensenada

action produces a dramatic geyser, and the secluded beach of Punta Banda. Near by are the surfers' favourites of San Miguel, Tres Marías, California and La Joya.

GUERRERO NEGRO

Although ostensibly a dull town of endless saltflats, vats and warehouses, Guerrero Negro is also the entry point to the Laguna Ojo de Liebre (Scammon's Lagoon), a protected national park where grey whales come to breed between December and March. Lookout posts dot the shore and skiffs can be rented at the beach.

> ### Did you know ?
>
> *From December to March, the warm lagoon waters of Ojo de Liebre and San Ignacio see the courting, mating and breeding of some 20,000 grey whales that swim south from the Bering Sea.*

HERMOSILLO

The industrialised city of Hermosillo appears to have little charm, yet its strategic site, 225km south of the border town of Nogales on Highway 15, with easy access to the beach resorts of Guaymas and Bahía Kino, about 100km west, makes it a good stop-over. The attractive colonial heart centres around the shady Plaza de Zaragoza, flanked by the Catedral and the Palacio de Gobierno. South of here lies the Centro Ecológico de Sonora, a zoo and botanical garden full of indigenous and desert specimens.

On the slopes of the Cerro de la Campaña, a hill overlooking the town, is the **Museo Regional de Sonora** in a converted penitentiary and, further north, the Ciudad Universitario, with its museum of local sericulture.

🔲 28A4
❓ Whale-watching tours:
Ecogrupos de México,
Avenida Insurgentes Sur
1971, Mexico City, DF
01020 ☎ (5) 661 9121;
fax: 662 7354 ⏰ Jan–Apr

🔲 28B4
ℹ️ Palacio de Gobierno,
Edificio Norte, Paseo Río
Sonora ☎ (62) 170044

Museo Regional de Sonora
✉️ Jesús García Finál, corner
Estéban Sarmiento
☎ (62) 131234
⏰ Wed–Sat 10–5:30, Sun
10–3:30
🎫 Moderate; free Sun

A Drive through Southern Baja

This drive circles the southern tip of Baja California, passing through dramatic sierra and tiny villages, with a night stop at Los Cabos.

From La Paz drive south on Highway 1 before taking the left fork at San Pedro. From here the road winds up to El Triunfo.

Rich silver veins were discovered here in 1862, leading to a population explosion till the mines closed down in 1926. The town is

Whiling away the afternoon in the sleepy former silver-mining town of El Triunfo

now virtually a ghost town though small-scale mining has resumed.

Continue 8km to San Antonio, a farming and former silver-mining town, before twisting up into the Sierra El Triunfo. The road descends again to the coast at Los Barriles, renowned for its spectacular winds.

Stop here for a refreshing swim in the Bahía de las Palmas before lunch.

The road skirts the coast before twisting inland and climbing past small villages. About 4km beyond Santiago it crosses the Tropic of Cancer, marked by a concrete sphere. At Las Casitas, the road widens to descend to San José del Cabo (▶ 52), an ideal night-stop. Next morning, head for Cabo San Lucas along the coastal highway and drive to the marina.

Distance
397km

Time
2 days

Start/end point
La Paz
✚ 28B3

Lunch
Hotel Palmas de Cortés (££)
✉ Conocido en Los Barriles
☎ (112) 10050

Stop here for a glass-bottomed boat trip around the striking rock formation known as El Arco (The Arch).

Drive out of town on Highway 1 to Todos Santos, 80km to the north.

This quiet farming town is attracting a growing community of Americans and a small arts and crafts industry. Beautiful Playa Punta Lobos and Playa San Pedrito are just east of town. From here another 80km brings you back to La Paz.

The restored 1752 Jesuit church in Loreto has survived several earthquakes

LORETO ⭐⭐

Loreto, the first capital of the Californias, has a population of only 9,000, making it a peaceful getaway in a beautiful setting, backed by the Sierra de la Giganta. The modest town centre claims the well-conserved Jesuit mission, from where Father Junípero Serra set out in 1769 to establish a chain of 17 Californian missions. Inside, the **Museo de los Misiones** gives an informative introduction to local missionary activities. Around the church is a pedestrian area leading down to the harbour and beach where Loreto's few hotels are located. Activities include tennis at one of the world's most modern tennis centres, sport fishing, hiking and scuba diving, as well as boat trips to the lovely Isla Coronado. A mega-resort is planned 20km south at Puerto Loreto.

 28B3

Museo de los Misiones
- ✉ Salvatierra 16
- ☎ (113) 50441
- 🕐 Mon–Fri 10–4
- 🍴 Cafés (£) in nearby plaza
- ♿ Good
- 💲 Cheap

MULEGÉ ⭐

The sleepy oasis town of Mulegé overlooks the mouth of the 40km-long Bahía de Concepción, backed by the Sierra de Santa Lucía. The original settlement was founded beside Baja's only navigable river, whose water has nourished large groves of olive trees and date palms. On the hilltop above stands the 1705 Mision de Santa Rosalía, once an open prison and now the Museo de Mulegé, with an eclectic range of exhibits including old diving and mining equipment. Low-key Mulegé mainly attracts sport fishermen, but also offers kayaking upriver or to outlying islands, scuba diving, and jeep or horseback trips to see the Cuevas de San Borjita paintings.

 28A3
- ❓ Kayaking and cave-painting tours through Hotel Hacienda, Calle Romero Rubio, Mulegé
- ☎ (115) 30021
- 💲 Moderate

📍 28B3

ℹ️ Carretera al Norte Km 5.5
   ☎ (112) 40424. Small
   office on Tourist Wharf,
   Paseo Alvaro Obregón
   2130, 🕐 Mon–Sat

Museo de Antropología

✉️ Calle Altamirano corner 5
   de Mayo

☎ (112) 20162

🕐 Mon–Fri 9–6

🍴 Cafés and restaurants (£)
   on Plaza Constitución

♿ Few

🎫 Free

*Late afternoon sun floods
the beach, boats and
malecón at La Paz*

LA PAZ ✪✪

The prosperous capital of Baja California Sur (south Baja),
La Paz, lies on a large bay opening on to the Mar de
Cortés, an ecologically rich gulf dotted with island nature
reserves. Protected to the north by the peninsula of El
Monogote, whose shores are increasingly targeted by
resort hotels, downtown La Paz looks directly west
across the bay. This provides a major natural feature –
dramatic sunsets.

La Paz (ironically meaning 'peace') suffered a turbulent
past, set in motion by Hernán Cortés in 1535. Vicious
conflicts with the indigenous inhabitants were exacerbated
over the centuries by droughts, famines, smallpox, pirates,
American troops during the Texan War and, in 1853, the
infamous William Walker, intent on installing slavery. As a
result, no indigenous groups survived in Baja. The town's
fortunes were revived partly thanks to American sport
fishermen, ferry services, the Transpeninsular highway and
its free-port status, so that today La Paz boasts one of
Mexico's highest per-capita incomes.

The centre of La Paz radiates from Plaza Constitución,
where the Palacio de Gobierno faces the picturesque 19th-
century Catedral de la Señora de la Paz, built on the site of
a 1720 mission. Close by is the Teatro de la Ciudad, where
modern facilities include art galleries and a library. La Paz's
history is covered at the **Museo de Antropología**, where
informative displays illustrate Baja geology, the early
Pericue, Cochimi and Guaicura inhabitants and information
on the cave paintings near San Ignacio (➤ opposite).

The balmy climate averaging 25°C, constant breezes
and scenic palm-fringed *malecón* (seafront promenade)
make La Paz a relaxing base for exploring the inland sierra,
indulging in endless watersports or boat trips, or enjoying

58

the fine white sand of its beaches. The modernised town centre has few historical sights, but Baja is, after all, about the great outdoors.

Although the primary winter (January–March) grounds for humpback whales are around Los Cabos, they sometimes venture into the Bay of La Paz. Year-round boat trips go to Isla Partida, a seal sanctuary, and the islands of Cerralvo and Espíritu Santo, both nature reserves that offer diving and swimming in the transparent waters of their coves. Sport fishing meanwhile takes advantage of the 850 species of fish in the warm waters of the gulf.

> ### Did you know ?
>
> *No fewer than 120 species of cactus inhabit the Baja landscape, from miniature cushions to gigantic 20m-high cardons. In March and April their upper branches blossom with white flowers. Also common are the organ-pipe cactus, mainly in southern Baja, and the barrel cactus, which can serve as an emergency water source.*

SAN FELIPE ✪

Running from the border town of Mexicali, Highway 5 ends at San Felipe, a fishing village that has now mushroomed into a resort. The main reason to come here is for the prolific fishing. San Felipe also attracts beach-lovers, as its golden sands border the warm Mar de Cortés (as opposed to the chillier and rougher Pacific). Impressive tides make the beach south of town a popular target for dune-buggying, and this is where an increasing number of up-market hotels are appearing.

🔳 28A4
ℹ️ Mar de Cortés corner Manzanillo
🕐 Tue–Sun 9–2, 4–6

SAN IGNACIO ✪✪

This attractive oasis town on the edge of the monotonous Desierto de Vizcaíno makes a tranquil stop-over as well as being the entry point to Laguna San Ignacio, a major whale-watching spot 70km away. The little town itself features a shady plaza, a mission church (1786), a small **ethnographic museum** and extensive date-palm groves planted by the Jesuits. Trips can be arranged to the lagoon during the whale season and all year into the nearby Sierra de San Francisco to see some of the 500 caves painted by the area's original inhabitants centuries ago (but they can only be reached by 4WD or horse- or mule-back).

🔳 28A3

Museo Pinturas Rupestres
🔲 Misión de San Ignacio
☎ (115) 40222
🕐 Tue–Sun 10–5
🎫 Moderate

An oasis in the desert – the mission town of San Ignacio still has immense charm

Pacific Mexico

Mexico's oldest beach playgrounds are located along the Pacific coastline between Mazatlán and Acapulco. This is where the country's most dramatic beaches are found, backed by the craggy outline of the Sierra Madre del Sur. Glitzy favourites such as Acapulco and Puerto Vallarta are now joined by Ixtapa-Zihuatanejo, a burgeoning twin resort, and quieter destinations such as San Blas and Barra de Navidad, which offer a more genuine Mexican atmosphere. Long tracts of coastline remain undeveloped, while short forays can be made inland to hill villages where church bells are the only interruption to a peaceful existence. Watersports are king in these deep blue waters that are sometimes unsuitable for swimming due to their treacherous currents. Acapulco and Puerto Vallarta are the places to go for nightlife, good restaurants and shopping.

'No American records survive, save in the vague traditions about 'white men' from the west, those mysterious 'snake peoples', regarding the voyages made across the Pacific to America by ancient Asian mariners. '

DONALD A MACKENZIE
Myths of Pre-Colombian America (c1910)

———————————— • ————————————

Local fishermen at the Pacific resort of Mazatlán

High-rises may line the bay but Acapulco is still a dramatic sight

Acapulco

A stunning sweep of bay heralded Acapulco's rise to fame in the 1950s, a revival of its 16th-century fortunes when it was developed by Cortés and his men as a port. In 1565 the first galleon set sail from Manila in the Philippines (then under Spanish rule) to Acapulco, marking the beginning of a flourishing trade route that saw the wealth of the Orient exchanged with that of Nueva España.

Craggy cliffs at the western end of the bay are the launch-pad for Acapulco's fearless divers

With an international airport and a fast toll road from Mexico City, Acapulco's fortunes are assured. Lining its 11km horseshoe bay are endless high-rise hotels, nightclubs, restaurants and a string of beaches where watersports and sun-worshipping set the tone. A concrete jungle or a steamy, sybaritic holiday playground? Opinions are divided, but every visitor is at least won over by the stunning scenery.

From the eastern headland of Playa Bruja, the Costera Miguel Alemán sweeps past a succession of facilities that include five golf courses, children's recreation parks, a crafts market and the San Diego Fort high above the old town, before the bay twists into a peninsula. To the west is the towering cliff of La Quebrada, where daredevil divers plunge into the waves, and beyond this the tranquil beach and Coyuca Lagoon at Pie de la Cuesta. Air-conditioned buses shuttle along the front, making travel easy. Family holidays are much helped by this excellent infrastructure, but remember that Acapulco is an oasis in one of Mexico's poorest states.

What to See in Acapulco

FUERTE DE SAN DIEGO ✪✪
Overlooking the lively, narrow streets of the old town is this striking stone fort, with panoramic views over the bay and mountains. It was completed in 1617 to protect the thriving port from pirate and buccaneer attacks (including England's notorious Sir Francis Drake). Today, it functions as the Museo Histórico, with interesting historical and ethnographic exhibits.

> ✚ 72C1
> ✉ Calle Morelos and Playa Hornitos
> ☎ (74) 823828
> 🕐 Tue–Sun 10–6
> ℹ Playa Los Hornos, Costera Miguel Alemán
> ☎ (74) 8691

ISLA LA ROQUETA ✪
A few hundred metres off the Peninsula de las Playas, this small island, reached by glass-bottomed boats from below the Fuerte de San Diego, offers relaxing respite from the main Costera. Cross the island to reach a small, secluded bay with a restaurant, or climb to the lighthouse. The waters are targeted by scuba divers, who come to see the underwater shrine of La Virgen Sumergida.

> ✚ 72C1
> ✉ Off Peninsula de las Playas

Tourist boats at the ready on Laguna Coyuca at Pie de la Cuesta

PIE DE LA CUESTA ✪✪
This long, narrow spit of land separating the Pacific from the mangrove and palm-fringed Laguna Coyuca is a favourite with waterskiers. Sunset fanatics home in on the beach to watch the painted sky from a beach bar hammock and sponsor daredevil locals to pit their strength against the thundering surf. Sadly, in 1997 Hurricane Pauline did extensive damage to this stretch and it will be some time before it regains its idyllic backdrop.

> ✚ 72C1
> ✉ 11km northwest of Acapulco

LA QUEBRADA ✪✪✪
Acapulco's high divers plunge over 40m from this cliff into the crashing surf of a narrow cove below. This sight is even more spectacular after sundown, when the last divers carry lighted torches as they plunge. Have dinner or a drink while you witness this carefully timed feat of bravura.

> ✚ 72C1
> ✉ Plaza La Glorias, El Mirador Hotel, La Mira
> 🕐 Daily at 1, 7:30, 8:30, 9:30, 10:30PM
> ♿ Good
> 🖐 Cheap

63

Freshly shucked oysters at one of Barra de Navidad's friendly beach restaurants

What to See in Pacific Mexico

BARRA DE NAVIDAD ★

 72A2
 60km south of Manzanillo

This picturesque fishing village developed only recently into an alternative beach resort to soulless Manzanillo, about 60km south. Built on a sandbar adjacent to a large lagoon, Barra de Navidad offers modest hotels and restaurants, and safe swimming in a scenic setting. A new luxury resort, a 27-hole golf course and a beach club with endless watersports activities have changed the sleepy pace but much damage was suffered during an earthquake in 1994.

IXTAPA-ZIHUATANEJO ★★

72B1
Motorboats run all day from Playa Quieta, Ixtapa's northern beach, or sail there with Yates del Sol from Puerto Mio marina
☎ (755) 42694
🍴 Seafood restaurants (£)
ℹ Ixtapa shopping centre
☎ (755) 31967/8

These twin resort towns are only 6km apart, yet have very different characters. Ixtapa is the modern half, its beachfront lined with high-rise hotels squeezed along the 3km white-sand Playa del Palmar. The wide bay dotted with tiny islands offers boat trips, windsurfing, waterskiing and diving, but swimming can be dangerous. When the waves are strong, head for Isla Ixtapa, where a secluded beach fronts a nature reserve. Ixtapa also offers excursions to lagoons, horse riding, sport fishing, golf and diving.

For some, the former fishing-village setting of Zihuatanejo, with forested headlands plunging into secluded bays, is preferable. Although it is a jazzed-up version of its former self, it offers more atmosphere and older, less pretentious hotels. The least attractive beach, Playa Principal, edges the old town, but beyond a headland to the southeast are Playa Madera, a family beach with economical hotels; Playa la Ropa, home to up-market hotels; and Playa Las Gatas, only accessible by boat. Other attractions are the scenic road winding high over the headland to Playa la Ropa, and a new walkway connecting the main town beach with Playa Madera.

A Walk in Puerto Vallarta

This walk winds through atmospheric cobbled streets and leads you across the Río Cuale to where the Mexican heart still beats.

Start at the church on the main square of Old Vallarta.

The curious crown that tops Nuestra Señora de Guadalupe is a replica of the hapless Empress Carlota's crown. It fell off in a 1994 earthquake, but is now perfectly restored.

Leave the church, turn right into Hidalgo and right again up Iturbide. Climb two steep blocks to Carranza and turn right.

At the end of this street on the left is the Callejón de los Tarques, crossed by the bridge that Elizabeth Taylor and Richard Burton built to connect their two houses. There is a lovely view south from the corner.

Return along Carranza as far as Corona. Turn left and walk two blocks downhill for another superb view, looking north. Walk along Matamoros for five blocks, then turn left at Libertad. This goes over the Río Cuale into Insurgentes. Turn left at Lázaro Cárdenas.

On your left is Santa Cruz (built 1902), a popular neighbourhood church.

Continue three blocks further to the Emiliano Zapata market on your right before turning left down Camichín. Climb a few steps at the end to a riverside road. Follow it into Áquiles Serdán and walk straight on, crossing Insurgentes, to Ignacio Vallarta, then turn right. This brings you to steps down on to the Isla Cuale below. Walk west towards the sea.

On your right is the small Museo del Cuale (➤ 66), with an interesting collection of pottery, sculptures and other artefacts from Jalisco, Narayit and Colima.

The heart of Old Vallarta surrounds the unmistakable campanile of Nuestra Señora de Guadalupe

Distance
3km

Time
2 hours

Start point
Nuestra Señora de Guadalupe, Old Vallarta
🚩 72A2

End point
Isla Cuale
🚩 72A2

Lunch
Caruso (£–££)
✉ Insurgentes 109 (by Río Cuale)
☎ (322) 22748

65

🔲 28B2

ℹ️ Edificio Banrural, Avenida Camarón Sábalo, corner Tiburón ☎ (69) 165160

Museo Arqueológico de Mazatlán

✉️ Sixto Osuna 76, Paseo Olas Altas

☎ (69) 853502

🕐 Tue–Sun 10–6

🍴 Cafés (£) on Plazuela Machado

♿ Few

💷 Cheap

Mexico's largest shrimp-fishing fleet is based at Mazatlán

🔲 72A2

ℹ️ Morelos 28a (corner of main square)

Museo del Cuale

✉️ Isla Cuale

🕐 Tue–Sat 10–3, 4–7, Sun 10–2

🍴 Cafés and restaurants (££) near by

♿ None

MAZATLÁN ✪

This sprawling, unsophisticated resort town is also the largest west coast port between Los Angeles and the Panama Canal, a factor that makes it less commercialised than Mexico's other resorts. Jutting out on a peninsula marked by three hills, its beaches stretch for about 8km, lined by a sea-wall promenade, the *malecón*, which ends at the headland lighthouse of Olas Altas. Behind this hill top lies the commercial port and old town, while to the far north, Mazatlán's Zona Hotelera monopolises the seafront.

Despite the influx of tourism, initially attracted by rich sport fishing, Mazatlán still depends on its fishing industry, with tuna-canning factories and shrimp-freezing plants supplied daily by Mexico's largest shrimp fleet. Fish aside, it offers great sports (golf, tennis, riding, watersports), boat trips to two islands with pristine beaches and an atmospheric old town centre with a gracious old theatre, cathedral and a small **archaeological museum**, which displays locally excavated artefacts.

PUERTO VALLARTA ✪✪✪

Ever expanding and ever popular, Puerto Vallarta is located on Mexico's largest bay, the Bahía de Banderas. It acquired international fame in 1964 when John Huston's film *The Night of the Iguana* hit the screens, with a hot background romance between Richard Burton and Elizabeth Taylor. At that time Vallarta was just a quaint little fishing village with cobbled streets and tile-roofed houses. Today this aspect still exists, as does a moody backdrop of thickly forested hills that sometimes plunge straight into the Pacific, but beyond are high-rise hotels and condos, a marina, hip nightclubs, cosmopolitan restaurants and a vast array of high-quality shops.

Developments are spreading fast at both ends of the bay, to Mismaloya in the south, where an underwater park lies around the outlying rocks of Los Arcos, and 18km north to the self-contained Nueva Vallarta. Boat trips spirit you to beauty spots such as Boca de Tomatlán, Yelapa or the Islas Marietas, off Punta Mita. Equally scenic are the roads through the hills, such as to El Tuito: horse riding or biking are a good alternative to jeeps.

Old Vallarta is still unsurpassed for atmosphere; don't miss the *malecón* and Río Cuale environs. An island at the mouth of this river is home to the **Museo del Cuale** (► 66), restaurants and craft shops while on its north bank is the *malecón*, town hall and idiosyncratic church. The backstreets here are packed with intriguing shops and art galleries. The liveliest town beach, day and night, is Playa Los Muertos, at the southern end of the town centre.

SAN BLAS ✪✪

If you have a good insect repellent and revel in sleepy, unspoilt seaside towns, then this is where to go. Surfing is the number-one activity here, closely followed by bird-watching in the mangrove-fringed estuaries and La Tovara lagoon. From November to March over 200 migrating species join the 150 native species. The bay was an important 16th- to 18th-century departure point for Spanish expeditions, and ruins from this period include the old Aduana (Custom's House), the hilltop Fuerte de Basilio and a 1769 church.

✚ 72A3

✉ 130km northwest of Puerto Vallarta

Top: *Playa Mismaloya, location of* Night of the Iguana, *which propelled Puerto Vallarta to fame* Above: *the guardian angel of fishermen on Vallarta's* malecón

67

In the Know

If you only have a short time to visit Mexico, or would like to get a real flavour of the country, here are some ideas:

10
Ways to Be a Local

Squeeze lime on your food at every opportunity – allegedly, it kills bacteria .

When it's hot, spend the afternoon hours inside, in a shaded hammock or under a *palapa*.

Wear a hat: rancho-style in the north, Panama-style in the south.

Light a candle to the Virgen de Guadalupe.

Eat *tortillas* as if there is no tomorrow.

Be generous with *pesos* to street artists and adult beggars.

Take provisions with you on long bus trips: express buses do not always stop.

In Mexico City, after dark only use radio-taxis (*sitios*).

Haggle for local crafts at markets.

Be patient at every turn; the Mexican sense of time is very different, as you will learn.

10
Good Places to Have Lunch

Beto's Condesa (££) ✉ Playa Condesa, Costera Miguel Aleman, Acapulco ☎ (74) 840100/840473. Popular beachfront restaurant where you have the tantalising choice between lobster and succulent steaks.

Caesar's (££) ✉ Emiliano Zapata, corner Benito Juárez, Loreto ☎ (113) 30203. Bustling seafood restaurant in centre of Loreto: a must for anyone in the area.

Café del Bosque (££) ✉ Off Paseo de la Reforma, Bosque de Chapultepec, Mexico City ☎ (5) 516 4214. Lakeside restaurant in Chapultepec Park. Mexican and

international dishes with live *marimba* music.

Café la Glorida (££) ✉ Vicente Suárez 41, corner Amatlan, Colonia Condesa, Mexico City ☎ (5) 211 4180. In the arty, leafy quarter of Colonia Condesa. Informal, popular lunch spot with pavement tables serving international cuisine. Young, colourful clientele.

El Anclote (£–££) ✉ Playa El Anclote, Punta Mita, Puerto Vallarta ☎ (322) 21949. Flee to the northernmost headland of Bahía de Banderas for the ultimate beachside lunch. Seafood soup, beef, chicken or fresh lobster.

El Tule (£££) ✉ Hotel Victoria, Lomas del Fortin 1, Oaxaca ☎ (951) 52633. Panoramic hotel restaurant on the hillside. Regional specialities and international cuisine.

Gran Café del Portal (£) ✉ Independencia, corner Zamora, Veracruz ☎ (29) 312759. A Veracruz institution, founded in 1810 as La Parroquia. Breakfasts extend into lunches; much favoured by local dignitaries.

La Casona (££) ✉ Calle 60, No 434, Mérida ☎ (99) 238348. Beautifully restored mansion with attractive patio and garden for cool lunches. Italian cuisine.

Left: *resting in the desert sunshine*
Right: *horse riding along a rough, steep track*

Los Patos (££)

✉ Constitución 104, Oaxaca ☎ (951) 61704. Uninhibited views of Santo Domingo from the top terrace which is only open at lunch. Sophisticated Oaxacan dishes.

Restaurant Bella Italia (£)

✉ Hernandez Macias 50, San Miguel de Allende ☎ (415) 24989. Sunny garden courtyard for devouring delicious Italian dishes away from shopaholic crowds.

Observing underwater wonders with snorkel and mask

Kayaking across the Bahía de Banderas, off Puerto Vallarta

Swimming with dolphins on Isla Mujeres or on Cozumel

Top Activities

Horseback riding in Baja California's Sierra de la Giganta or in the hills around Oaxaca

Whale-watching (Dec–Apr) in Baja California

Rocking along in the Chihuahua–Pacífico Copper Canyon train

Watching the divers at La Quebrada, Acapulco

Parasailing at Acapulco, Ixtapa, Cancún or Puerto Vallarta

Hooking a marlin in the Mar de Cortés

Diving in the Caribbean at Los Manchones, off Isla Mujeres

Playing golf at the new 18-hole course designed by Jack Nicklaus at Cabo del Sol, Los Cabos

Top Handicraft Buys

- Handblown glass from Tonalá, Guadalajara
- Decorative tinwork from Oaxaca
- Silver jewellery and tableware from Taxco
- Handwoven textiles from Chiapas and Oaxaca
- Talavera ceramics from Puebla or cheaper look-alikes from Dolores Hidalgo

Best Baroque Churches

- Capilla del Rosario in Puebla's Santo Domingo
- Templo de la Valenciana in Guanajuato
- Santa Clara and Santa Rosa in Querétaro
- Santo Domingo in Oaxaca
- Santo Domingo in San Cristóbal

Best Fruits, Fresh or in Drinks

- *Guanabana*, soursop (related to the custard-apple)
- *Piña*, pineapple
- *Papaya*, pawpaw, eaten doused in lime juice
- *Mango*, but not the green variety used for preserves
- *Naranja*, orange, delicious in juices when mixed with *mandarina* (mandarin) or *zanahoria* (carrot)

Best Climbs

- Iztaccíhuatl, the sister volcano to Popocatépetl, for a close-up on Popo's rising steam
- The church of Nuestra Señora de Los Remedios, atop the largest pyramid in the Americas at Cholula
- The Pirámide de la Luna at Teotihuacán for a clear view of early town-planning
- Cheat at Taxco and take the cable-car up to Monte de Taxco
- The giant statue of Morelos on the island of Janitzio overlooking Lago de Pátzcuaro
- El Faro (the lighthouse) at Mazatlán, the world's second-highest natural lighthouse after Gibraltar
- The Faro Viejo at Cabo San Lucas, for panoramic ocean views
- Nohuch Mul at Cobá, the tallest pyramid on the northern Yucatán peninsula, for sweeping jungle views
- The Torre Latino-americana in Mexico City: another cheat as you'll be in a lift
- El Castillo, at the heart of Chichén Itzá

The South

Indigenous people account for over 75 per cent of the population, adding a clear visual presence to this region. Beyond apparently deserted hills are villages with firmly entrenched customs and craft traditions. Hugging the coast to the north is the state of Veracruz, land of riotous February carnivals and *marimba* bands that impart a distinctly tropical, almost Caribbean atmosphere. Oaxaca, to the south, remains queen of history, archaeology, culture and crafts. East of Veracruz is the oil-rich state of Tabasco, once the heart of Mesoamerica's oldest civilisation, the Olmecs, but now clearly a front-runner in fast-developing Mexico. Furthest south is the troubled region of Chiapas, where indigenous people have suffered at the hands of landowners and economic interests for centuries. This, too, is where high, pine-clad mountains alternate with tropical rainforests that conceal evocative Mayan ruins.

'Luxuriant vegetation of emerald hue bends in flower–laden branches to the waters' edge, overarched by a sky of purest azure; brilliant–hued butterflies and humming–birds with metallic sheen fly from flower to flower…'

TEOBERT MALER
Memoirs of the Peabody Museum (1908–10)

———————— • ————————

The interior of the Templo de Santo Domingo, jewel of Oaxaca

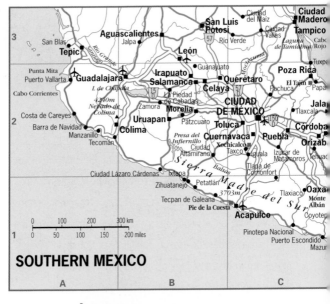

SOUTHERN MEXICO

Oaxaca

Oaxaca, capital of the state of the same name, is a graceful, small-scaled city where the sun seems to shine permanently on the distant hills. Unique, colourful and full of surprises, it is one of Mexico's most relaxed, pleasurable towns. History is omnipresent yet not overpowering, while markets, art galleries, craft shops, cafés and restaurants make for endless tempting distractions.

At Oaxaca's heart is a magnificent zócalo rimmed by cafés, and a genuine crossroads for anyone in town – resident, visitor or shoeshiner alike. Once the centre for the Mixtec and Zapotec civilisations, Oaxaca rapidly developed a strong Spanish flavour after it was conquered in 1533. Countless churches (including the masterful baroque Santo Domingo), elegant mansions, government buildings, decorative grille-work and charming plazas were built, creating a harmonious backdrop for the strikingly proud indigenous population.

In 1987 Oaxaca, together with Monte Albán, a fabulous legacy of the Zapotecs (➤ 20) was declared a world

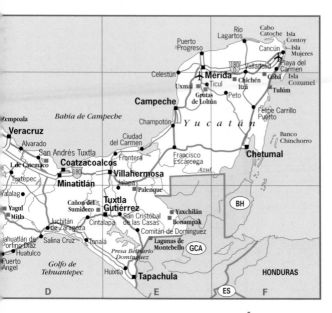

heritage site by UNESCO, and since then seems not to have looked back. Excellent services, atmospheric hotels and a network of craft villages have all been organised and made accessible, offering a wide choice of activities to the visitor. The silhouette of the Sierra Madre del Sur is a constant reminder of its rural attractions, whether on horseback, bicycle or by car. However Oaxaca's charm is best enjoyed through strolls through cobbled streets, past brightly painted houses brimming with flowers, peeping into churches or courtyards, checking out shops, or people-watching on the zócalo.

Benito Juárez market in Oaxaca

What to See in Oaxaca

MUSEO REGIONAL DE OAXACA

Next door to Santo Domingo is the former Dominican monastery that now houses the regional museum, backed by a newly landscaped botanical garden. The rooms and vaulted cloisters of this building display the wealth of archaeological artefacts found in the state. Pride of place goes to the fantastic collection of Mixtec jewellery found in Tomb 7 at Monte Albán, including gold, turquoise, rock-crystal, jade and silver.

MUSEO RUFINO TAMAYO ✪✪

The late Rufino Tamayo, one of Mexico's foremost 20th-century painters and a native of Oaxaca, spent over 20 years collecting pre-Hispanic antiquities, and this small, select museum is the result. Five colour-coordinated rooms display some exceptional pieces, in particular those devoted to the Olmec, Occidente, Totonac and Maya cultures. Concerts and art exhibitions are also held here.

TEMPLO DE SANTO DOMINGO ✪✪

Started in the late 16th century, this church is one of Mexico's finest examples of baroque architecture. Above the main entrance is an extraordinary bas-relief genealogical tree of the family of Domingo de Guzmán, the 13th-century founder of the Dominican order. Beyond this, the soaring ceiling is entirely faced in elaborately gilded and painted stucco, surrounding 36 inset paintings. To the right is the Capilla del Rosario, another magnificent interpretation of Mexican baroque by indigenous artisans.

72C1
Ex-Convento de Santo Domingo, Alcalá
(951) 62991
Tue–Sat 10–6, Sun 10–5
García Vigil 517 and Reforma 526
Good
Moderate; free Sun

72C1
Morelos 503
(951) 64750
Wed–Sat, Mon 10–2, 4–7, Sun 10–3
Very good
Cheap

72C1
Alcalá, corner Gurrión
Daily 7–1, 5–8
Good
Free

Below: *an exhibit at Museo Rufino Tamayo*

Right: *the defensive style of the Templo de Santo Domingo was intended to deter attack*

74

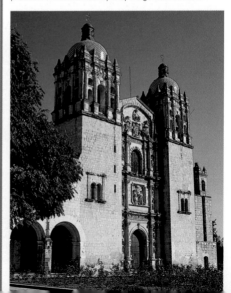

A Walk around Oaxaca

This walk through the colonial heart of Oaxaca takes in churches, museums and the city's inimitable atmosphere.

Start at the zócalo and head for the Catedral on the north side.

Built in 1533, it contains a bronze altar, antique organ and, best of all, an elaborate 18th-century baroque façade.

Leave the Catedral, turning sharp right, and walk along Independencia to the pedestrian street of Alcalá. Turn left and walk uphill to the Museo de Arte Contemporáneo. After visiting, continue uphill, turn right along Murguia as far as Cinco de Mayo, then turn left. On your right is the Camino Real Hotel.

This 400-year-old former convent of Santa Catalina, now a national monument, is very picturesque and exudes a distinctive atmosphere.

Continue uphill to Santo Domingo and visit both the church and adjacent museum. On leaving, turn right past the Instituto de Artes Gráficas to the Plazuela del Carmen Alto.

This small plaza is home to a colourful daily market of Oaxacan crafts.

Leave the plaza, turning left into García Vigil. Continue downhill for four blocks before turning right into Morelos. Two blocks further is the Museo Rufino Tamayo. After visiting, continue another two blocks.

On the left is the Basílica de la Soledad, a late-17th-century church, home to a statue of the town's patron saint and a small museum.

Walk down the steps to Independencia. Turn left and walk four blocks east to the church of San Felipe Neri.

This church (1636) is noted for its fine frescoed walls and ornately gilded altar and nave.

Continue along Independencia to the zócalo.

Distance
2km

Time
3 hours including stops

Start/end point
Zócalo
✚ 72C1

Lunch
Café del Instituto de Artes Gráficas (£)
✉ Alcalá 507
☎ (951) 66980

Oaxaca's treasure-trove of crafts is hard to bypass

A Drive in Oaxaca Valley

This drive covers the valley southeast of the state capital, taking in crafts villages and archaeological sites.

Leave Oaxaca by following signs to Istmo or Tehuantepec, which bring you to Highway 190. You soon enter the village of El Tule, with its colourful church and giant tree.

This gnarled *ahuehuete* tree is claims to be the world's largest tree with a circumference of 58m; it is thought to be some 2,000 years old and is still sprouting.

Continue 6km on the highway to a turn-off on the right to Tlacochuaya.

The ridges and whorls of the venerable ahuehuete *(cypress) tree in El Tule*

Here a magnificent church stands within a Dominican monastery complex, its interior notable for ornate floral murals and a 16th-century organ.

Return to the highway, continue east, stopping at the archaeological site of Dainzú before turning left to Teotitlán del Valle, famed for its hand–woven rugs. Return and continue along the highway to another turn–off on the left to Yagul.

This little-visited Zapotec site sits high in the cacti-studded hills and offers fabulous 360-degree views of the valley. Its ball court is the second largest in Mesoamerica.

Follow the highway to a junction: take the left fork to Mitla. Drive into the village plaza.

Visit the Frissell Museum before walking uphill past numerous crafts outlets to the red-domed church, crafts market and the superb Zapotec structures (▶ 77).

Continue east from Mitla to a turn-off to Hierve del Agua. An unsurfaced road leads to this sensational site: a petrified waterfall and pools. Return to Oaxaca by the same route.

Distance
120km

Time
5–6 hours, depending on stops

Start/end point
Oaxaca
 72C1

Lunch
Centeotl (£)
✉ Zona Arqueológica Yagul
☎ (956) 20289

What to See in the South

HUATULCO (▶ 19, TOP TEN)

MAZUNTE
This delightful, low-key fishing village lies 62km west of Huatulco, between Puerto Angel and Puerto Escondido. A beautiful adjoining beach, San Agustinillo, is a favourite among Mexicans for long lunches under shady *palapas*. Outlying rocks shelter the beach, making it ideal for those in search of calm waters and fresh seafood. Mazunte itself is home to the world's only turtle research centre and museum (**Museo de la Tortuga**), an impressive modern set-up with turtles representing 9 of the world's 11 types. The wild 15km beach north of here, not accessible by road, sees the arrival of some 200,000 Olive Ridley turtles during their nesting season, from July to December. Mazunte is also home to a local enterprise making natural cosmetics.

MITLA
Meaning 'place of the dead', this fascinating Zapotec site was occupied between AD 400 and 700 but then became solely a ceremonial centre. Much of the rich stone-carving was finished by the later Mixtecs, who alternated with the Zapotecs in regional power until the Spanish arrived in 1521. The structures are famed for their complex geometrical stonework, made using an inlay technique. This is particularly well preserved in the Grupo de las Columnas, which contains the masterful Patio de las Grecas. Near by, another patio structure incorporates two underground cruciform tombs.

The remains of Mixtec murals are displayed in the grounds of the red-domed 16th-century church that rises above the site. Behind it is a large crafts market. The village is dominated by small crafts shops and *mezcal* bars, but don't miss the Frissell Museum, on the plaza at the entrance.

MONTE ALBÁN (▶ 20, TOP TEN)

Zapotec stone inlay techniques created 14 different patterns on the palaces and tombs of Mitla

72C1

Museo de la Tortuga
- On main road (Mex 200)
- (958) 43055, fax: 43063
- Tue–Sat 10–4:30, Sun 10–2:30
- Excellent seafood restaurants (£) in Playa San Agustinillo
- None
- Cheap

73D1
- Highway 190, 45km from Oaxaca
- Daily 8–5
- Cafés and restaurants (£) in village
- Few
- Cheap; free Sun

PALENQUE (➤ 22, TOP TEN)

PUERTO ÁNGEL

This charming fishing port, nestling between forested hills, has long been a favourite of those in the know. However, in 1997 Hurricane Pauline caused extensive damage, and although reconstruction was rapid, some scars still remain.

There is little to do here except lap up the sun, lazing on the pretty Playa Panteon and watching diving pelicans, but the slow pace is appealing and the locals are extremely friendly. Ultra-fresh seafood is provided by fishermen who beach their boats or moor at the jetty. Four kilometres northwest is the hippy beach of Zipolite, where thatched beach huts again suffered from the hurricane, but the 3km of white sands ending in rocky headlands still attract backpackers, while surfers revel in the often wild waves. Currents are dangerous and drownings have occurred.

PUERTO ESCONDIDO

Of the three beach resorts scattered along the Oaxacan coast, Puerto Escondido takes the middle road between sophisticated Huatulco and relaxed Puerto Ángel. Its fishing-village past has receded somewhat with the influx of hotels, restaurants and shops, but the lovely curved bay is only the beginning: to the east lie palm-fringed Playa Marinero and the surfers' paradise of Playa Zicatela, while to the west is the pretty cove of Puerto Ángelito, accessible by boat or road. From Playa Principal a walkway winds around the cliffs, offering sweeping sea views. Nightlife thrives, too, in the form of low-key beach bars.

 73D1
✉ 83km southeast of Puerto Escondido
🍴 Restaurant Susy (£), Playa del Panteon

The relaxed fishing village of Puerto Ángel

✚ 72C1
✉ 264km south of Oaxaca
ℹ Boulevard Benito Juárez s/n, Fraccionamiento Bacocho ☎ (958) 20175/20537

SAN CRISTOBAL DE LAS CASAS ✪✪✪

This beautiful but politically troubled town, high in the forested hills east of Tuxtla, remains a prime tourist favourite. Wood smoke fills the air in the narrow cobbled streets, shops offer an amazing array of local crafts, and hotels and restaurants are reasonable. Unfortunately, since the Zapatistas' uprising of 1994 events have proved that little is being done to improve rural conditions, an ongoing problem for centuries.

The main sights in town are the restored cathedral on the main square and, uphill on Avenida General Utrilla, the fabulous church of Santo Domingo (1547). Transformed in the 18th century, it presents a lacy, carved façade and an ornate baroque interior. Its terraces throng with an impromptu crafts market daily, while the adjoining monastery houses the **Museo Regional** and the fascinating weavers' co-operative, **Sna Jolobil**. The latter displays and sells examples of the skilled techniques still practised by local communities. Handicrafts continue two blocks north at the labyrinthine Mercado. East of here is Na-Bolom, a fascinating institution founded by Frans Blom and his wife Trudy. They both extensively researched and supported local communities, leaving this house as a legacy to anthropologists and writers, who stay here.

San Cristóbal is also the starting point for excursions to local villages. San Juan Chamula, 9km north, has a large Sunday market in front of its extraordinary church. Here the Tzotzils carry on a form of worship that combines Christianity with ancient Mayan spiritual practices. Entry to the church is not allowed during religious ceremonies.

🔲 73E1
ℹ️ Delegacion de Turismo, Avenida Miguel Hidalgo 2
☎ (967) 86570

Museo Regional
✉️ Ex-Convento de Santo Domingo
☎ (967) 81609
🕐 Tue–Sun 9–4
♿ None
💵 Cheap; free Sun

Sna Jolobil
✉️ Ex-Convento de Santo Domingo
☎ (967) 82646
🕐 Mon–Sat 9–2, 4–6:30
♿ None
💵 Free

San Cristobal's Dominican church combines vast scale with ornately carved vegetal motifs

✚ 73E1
ℹ Belisario Domínguez 950
☎ (961) 39396/9

Museo Regional
✉ Parque Madero
☎ (961) 34479
🕐 Tue–Sun 9–5
🍴 Cafés (£) in park
♿ Good
🎫 Cheap; free Sun

*The vertiginous depths of
the Cañon de Sumidero*

TUXTLA GUTIÉRREZ ✪

Although not an essential attraction in itself, Tuxtla is at the crossroads of several outstanding southern destinations. This modern capital of the state of Chiapas lies in a hot saucer rimmed by hills that rise in the east to San Cristóbal de las Casas. In the town centre is the Parque Madero, a cultural complex containing a theatre, botanic gardens and the **Museo Regional**, which has a good display of Olmec and Mayan artefacts. To the south is a unique and enlightened zoo (► 111).

Seventeen kilometres east, on Highway 190, is Chiapa de Corzo, Chiapas' first Spanish settlement, dating from 1528. The arcaded main square encloses an extraordinary fountain structure, La Pila, built to resemble the Spanish crown. One block away looms the vast church of Santo Domingo, whose former convent now houses the Museo de la Laca (lacquer museum), a local craft speciality. Just behind flows the Río Grijalva. From the *embarcadero* (jetty) boats leave for tours of the Cañon de Sumidero. This awesome canyon, with depths of over 1,000m, can also be viewed from lookout points along a road north of Tuxtla.

VERACRUZ ◑◑

Known above all for its riotous Shrovetide carnival, Veracruz was also the place where Hermán Cortés and his men first landed in 1519. This major port on the Gulf of Mexico later witnessed the arrival of French forces in 1838, and in 1847 was bombarded by the Americans. As a result, many of its monuments date from the late 19th century, with the exception of the beautiful **Fortaleza de San Juan de Ulua**, built in the 16th century and later much extended. Lying north of town in the main port area, the fort's sturdy walls and bastions, which once enclosed a political prison and presidential palace, now contain a museum.

Life in central Veracruz revolves around the Plaza de Armas, flanked by the Catedral (1734) and the fine Palacio Municipal (1627), where hawkers vie with *marimba* bands long into the steamy night. The aquarium (► 111) is also exceptional, but for swimming head south to the popular, though dirty, Mocambo beach, near Boca del Río.

VILLAHERMOSA ◑

The modern, oil-rich city of Villahermosa is famed, above all, for its relics of the sophisticated Olmec civilisation, Mesoamerica's oldest. A large leisure complex, the Centro de Investigaciones de las Culturas Olmecas (CICOM), includes exceptional Olmec pieces at its Museo de Antropología, but it is at the **Parque Nacional de La Venta** that you will see the impressive giant heads that were hauled here from their original site at La Venta, 95km away. These now sit in a lush, wooded area that also houses an excellent zoo of local Tabasco animals. More insights into local nature lie at Yumka, a well-organised 100-hectare jungle, savannah and lagoon refuge for many endangered species (► 111).

An Olmec bas-relief at the open-air Parque Nacional de La Venta, just outside Villahermosa

---

➕ 73D2

Fortaleza de San Juan de Ulua
⊠ Islote de San Juan de Ulúa
☎ (29) 385751/385151
🕐 Tue–Sun 9:30–5
🍴 Drinks available
♿ Few
💲 Expensive

➕ 73E2
ℹ️ Edificio Tabasco, Paseo Tabasco 1504 ☎ (93) 163633

Parque Nacional de La Venta
⊠ Boulevard Adolfo Ruiz Cortines
🕐 Tue–Sun 9–8
🍴 Cafeteria (£)
♿ Good
💲 Cheap; free Sun

The Yucatán Peninsula

Jutting out between the Gulf of Mexico and the Caribbean is a flat limestone shelf riddled with underground rivers, caves and *cenotes* (sinkholes). Above ground this peninsula is less than inspiring, consisting mainly of monotonous savannah and low jungle. Yet it continues to attract charter-loads of visitors. The reason is quite simple: this was the heartland of the great Maya culture and, along with Guatemala, claims their most astonishing monuments. Chichén Itzá, Uxmal, Cobá and Tulum, as well as countless lesser-known sites, are a magnet for the historically inclined visitor. And beyond them lie the aquamarine depths of the Caribbean, where underwater life is hard to surpass. Lining the coast is a string of resorts, starting with Cancún, that cater for every touristic and hedonistic whim.

> *'I saw unexpectedly a spectacle of extraordinary beauty ... a large cavern or grotto, with a roof of broken, overhanging rock, high enough to give an air of wilderness and grandeur.'*
>
> JOHN LLOYD STEPHENS
> *Incidents of Travel in the Yucatan*
> (1841)

———•———

Stone motifs of sky serpent masks adorn the façade of Uxmal's Cuadrángulo de las Monjas (the Nunnery)

ℹ Calle 59 No 514,
between Calle 62 and 64

Mérida

The elegant capital of the state of Yucatán makes a relaxed base for exploring major Mayan ruins such as Chichén Itzá (► 17) and Uxmal (► 89). Mérida has a strong sense of history and culture, much of which has been absorbed from its links with the US, Cuba, Europe and even the Middle East. This unusually cosmopolitan flavour expanded further in the 1950s when direct road and rail links were established with Mexico City.

Despite enormous hardship, the Maya still find time to smile

When the Spaniards arrived in 1542, led by Francisco de Montejo, they used the stones of the declining Mayan city of T'ho to erect their cathedral and administrative structures. But it was not until the late 19th century that Mérida's fortunes really changed. The catalyst was the burgeoning sisal industry, whose prosperous French investors bequeathed an impressive *belle époque* architectural style. Today, many of the earlier colonial buildings around the zócalo have been restored, while to the north the tree-lined Paseo de Montejo is home to a string of grandiose edifices that were the residences of the sisal-empire builders. This area is now regarded as 'modern' Mérida, targeted by airline offices, large hotels and nightclubs.

South of the zócalo, in the streets surrounding the sprawling market, is a more mundane but authentic quarter, where everywhere you will see diminutive Mayan women in embroidered white dresses and older gentlemen in their immaculate white *guayaberas* (tucked shirts).

What to See in Mérida

CASA DE MONTEJO ✪✪
This is Mérida's first Spanish house, built in 1549 by the conquistador Francisco de Montejo. His descendants lived there until only a few years ago, but today the mansion more prosaically houses a branch of Banamex. The façade remains an outstanding example of the Plateresque style, with sculpted busts and the Montejo coat of arms depicting two soldiers triumphing over the bodies of prostrate Maya.

CATEDRAL DE SAN ILDEFONSO ✪✪
Built between 1556 and 1599, this is said to be the oldest cathedral on the American continent, although Campeche's inhabitants would not agree. The massive edifice was built with the stones of the dismantled Mayan town of T'ho, but during the 1915 Revolution it was stripped bare. Today's worshippers venerate an impressive 7m-tall statue of Christ that dominates the lofty stone interior. Other sights flanking the main square outside are the Palacio Municipal (1735) opposite, and the Palacio de Gobierno (1892) on the northern side, whose interior displays a remarkable series of 27 paintings depicting the complex history of the Maya, Spaniards and Mexicans.

MUSEO DE ANTROPOLOGÍA E HISTORIA ✪✪
Located on Mérida's most salubrious avenue, this elaborate 1911 mansion was built for the state governor to rival others belonging to prosperous sisal barons. As a result, the interior Doric columns, marble, chandeliers and extravagant mouldings somewhat overpower the exhibits. These offer a clear background to the history of the Yucatán, its Mayan sites and culture. Artefacts include a rare collection of jade offerings recovered from the *cenote* at Chichén Itzá.

Mérida's elegant Casa de Montejo

✚ 73F2
✉ Plaza Mayor, Calle 63
🍴 Cafés and restaurants (£–££) on square
 Free

✚ 73F2
✉ Plaza Mayor, Calle 60
🕐 Daily 6AM–8PM
🍴 Cafés and restaurants (£–££) on square and along Calle 60
♿ Few
 Free

✚ 73F2
✉ Palacio Canton, Paseo de Montejo 485
☎ (99) 230557
🕐 Tue–Sat 9–8, Sun 8–2
🍴 Cafés and restaurants (£–££) along Paseo de Montejo
♿ Few
 Moderate; free Sun

Campeche's impressive 2.5km of fortified walls were built to repel pirates

What to See in the Yucatán Peninsula

CAMPECHE ✪✪

Founded in the 1540s, Campeche suffered repeated attacks from pirates, and it was not until the erection of 3m-thick walls, reinforced by eight bastions, in the late 17th century that it prospered. There are two excellent museums and several interesting churches, including the Catedral on the main square and the 16th-century church of San Francisco. In the central Baluarte de la Soledad is a superb display of Mayan stelae, while to the south, in a **museum** in the hilltop Fuerte de San Miguel, is a rare collection of Mayan jade and pottery.

✚ 73E2
ℹ Calle 12 No 153, between Calle 55 and 53, also next to Catedral

Museo Histórico Fuerte de San Miguel
⊠ 4km south of Campeche
🕐 Tue–Sun 8:30–1, 2:15–7
♿ Good
🎟 Cheap

CANCÚN ✪

Chosen by computer as the site of Mexico's largest resort in the early 1970s, Cancún attracts over 2.5 million visitors annually to indulge in powdery white-sand beaches, high-rise hotels, endless entertainment, sports and shopping. This is hardly the 'real' Mexico, but makes an easy base for heading inland or further south along the increasingly developed 'Maya Riviera'. Most visitors come on package holidays and their 24-hour needs are well catered for. But long before the tourists came, there was a small Mayan settlement here: its remains are visible at the Ruinas del Rey and at the **Museo Arqueológico**.

✚ 73F3
ℹ Dirección de Turismo, Ayuntamiento, Avenida Tulum 5

Museo Arqueológico
⊠ Centro de Convenciones, Km 9, Boulevard Kukulcán
☎ (98) 830199
🕐 Tue–Sun 8–7
🍴 Cafés and restaurants (£–££) near by
♿ Good
🎟 Moderate; free Sun

CHICHÉN ITZÁ (► 17, TOP TEN)

COBÁ ✪✪

This important lakeside Mayan site remains little visited, despite its significance in the web of *sacbeob* (sacred 'white paths') connecting other historic sites. Only a tiny proportion of this enormous city has been excavated, and these ruins are scattered through the jungle, so bring sturdy shoes, water and insect repellent. Immediately visible is the Grupo de Cobá, whose narrow, steep

✚ 73F2
⊠ 42km northwest of Tulum
☎ (98) 324634
🕐 Daily 8–7
🍴 Cafés and restaurants (£)
🎟 Moderate; free Sun

pyramid rises over 30m above the tree-tops to give sweeping views over the lake. A ball court is next on the trail, followed by the Conjunto de las Pinturas (Temple of the Painted Ladies), some carved stelae and altars known as the Grupo Macanxoc. Nearly 3km further on towers 42m-high Nohoch Mul, the tallest pyramid in the northern Yucatán peninsula. A strenuous climb is rewarded by a small temple decorated with descending god figures.

COZUMEL ✪

Like Cancún, the island of Cozumel is almost entirely geared to the needs of tourists. Cruise ship passengers, scuba divers and Cancunites all come to taste the delights of the renowned Palankar Reef, one of the world's top diving destinations. Unfortunately the most visited beach, Chankanab, now offers mainly dead coral, although the fish are spectacular. Skilled divers make day trips to some 20 different sites further out. Good swimming beaches dot the southwestern corner of the island, but strong currents make the eastern coast dangerous. In the unspoilt north lies a late Mayan site, **San Gervasio**. The main town, San Miguel, is a modernised place, where, again, the flavour of real Mexico is virtually absent.

➕ 73F2
ℹ️ Plaza Cozumel, Avenida Juárez, between Avenida 5 and 10

San Gervasio
✉️ 13km northeast of San Miguel
📞 (98) 324634
🕐 Daily 8–5
⛴️ Frequent ferries from Playa del Carmen, boat trips from Cancún

Spectacular coral and shoals of brilliantly coloured fish have put Cozumel firmly on the diver's map

GRUTAS DE LOLTÚN ✪✪

These spectacular underground caves and galleries lie in the heart of the undulating Puuc Hills, south of Mérida. Inhabited over 2,500 years ago, their secret network was also used by rebellious Maya seeking refuge during the mid-19th-century Caste War. Fabulous rock formations, cave paintings, musical stalactites and the Cathedral, a large chamber that soars over 50m high, are all part of this compelling underworld.

➕ 73E2
✉️ 115km south of Mérida, 50km east of Uxmal
🕐 Daily guided tours at 9:30, 11, 12:30, 2, 3:30
🍴 Café (£) at entrance
♿ None
💷 Moderate

73F3

Rueda Medina, opposite jetty

Parque Nacional El Garrafón
✉ Carretera al Faro
☎ (987) 70318
🕐 Daily 9–4
🍴 Snack bar (£) on breezy terrace
♿ None
🖐 Moderate; free Sun

ISLA MUJERES

This delightful little island has a sleepy rhythm of its own. Most streets are of sand, cars are outnumbered by golf-carts and bicycles, and nights are tranquil. It makes an enticing escape from the over-development on Cancún, and as well as good beaches and diving, offers several attractions. The main town and services adjoin Playa Norte, while at the far southern tip is **El Garrafón**, a national park covering part of the Great Mayan Reef. Although the coral is dead, boat trips take snorkellers and divers to better spots further afield.

Half-way down the central lagoon lies Dolphin Discovery, a registered dolphin centre, near a turtle farm. A small altar to the fertility goddess Ixchel explains the island's name ('island of women'); when the Spanish first landed they found numerous crude statues of her. Day trips also go to Isla Contoy, an uninhabited bird sanctuary.

73F3
☎ Free info-line 1-800-GO-PLAYA

Rocky cliffs slope down to the sea at the southern tip of Isla Mujeres

PLAYA DEL CARMEN

Once a beach-bum's paradise, this small resort is mushrooming fast. The modern town centre is built on a narrow grid of streets bisected by Avenida 5, a favourite promenading and restaurant strip, ending at palm-fringed Caribbean beaches. South of the Cozumel ferry pier is an airstrip and golf course, while north of town hotels are rapidly eating up the shore. Nightlife, eating and shopping opportunities are plentiful, but there is little else.

73F2
✉ Highway 307
☎ (98) 324634
🕐 Daily 8–5
🍴 Snack bars (£) in plaza
♿ Few
🖐 Moderate; free Sun

TULUM

This dramatically sited Mayan ruin (AD 900–1500) rises perilously on a cliff edge north of a slowly expanding stretch of hotels. Inland lies a typical services town without much beauty but with reasonable prices. However, if you want a few quiet days sleeping beside the waves, Tulum's beach accommodation is ideal.

The ruins themselves are now fronted by a large

shopping plaza from where a tram ferries visitors to the site, although it is within easy walking distance. Sadly, this new structure has taken away much of Tulum's drama, but the Templo de los Frescos is still remarkable for its faded interior murals, the palace for its carved figures and the Castillo complex for its serpentine columns and sweeping sea views.

UXMAL

⭐⭐⭐

Uxmal was founded between the 5th and 6th centuries AD and at one point had some 25,000 inhabitants, before being abandoned around 900. It stands on a wide plateau in the Puuc Hills, near several smaller sites of similar style. Outstanding is the Pirámide del Adivino (Magician's Pyramid), an elliptical structure rising over 40m high. Immediately to the west stands the Cuadrángulo de las Monjas (The Nuns' Quadrangle), where fine stone inlay typifies the Puuc style. South of here is an elevated complex, the Palacio del Gobernador (Governor's Palace) showing unsurpassed decorative techniques. Beyond is the Casa de las Tortugas (House of the Turtles), the Gran Pirámide (Great Pyramid) and the Casa de la Vieja (Old Lady's House). Visitors with guides can see the last two structures where numerous sculpted phalluses at the Templo de los Falos (Temple of Phalluses) point to a unique cult in Uxmal.

Stone motifs on Uxmal's Cuadrángulo de las Monjas depict schematic Mayan huts and sky serpents

+ 73E2
✉ 78km south of Mérida on Highway 261
☎ (99) 249677
◷ Daily 8–5
🍴 Restaurant (£) in museum complex
♿ Few
▥ Moderate; free Sun
❓ Spectacular sound-and-light show at 7PM in Spanish, 9PM in English

Did you know ?

The sophisticated Mayan culture rose to prominence in the first centuries AD with the building of Palenque and other major sites in Guatemala, Belize and Honduras. Between AD 600 and 900 Chichén Itzá, Uxmal and Cobá reached their zenith, before being mysteriously abandoned. Over-population? Internal warfare? Drought? Hypotheses abound.

A Drive from Cancún to Cobá

Distance
350km

Time
9–10 hours (including stops)

Start/end point
Avenida López Portillo, Cancún
➕ 73F3

Lunch
Hotel María de la Luz (£)
✉ Plaza Principal, Valladolid
☎ (985) 62071

This drive takes you inland from Cancún to the colonial town of Valladolid and the Mayan site of Cobá. A dip in a *cenote* is an option.

Drive west out of Cancún along Avenida López Portillo following signs for Valladolid/Mérida. Avoid the cuota highway (a pricey tollroad, though quicker) and remain on the old Highway 180 which takes you through a string of pretty rural villages.

Traditional Mayan houses are generally elliptical in shape with tightly aligned tree-branch walls and *palapa* (thatched palm-leaf) roofs.

Drive 159km to Valladolid, watching out for the countless topes (speed-breakers) that pepper every village. Drive straight into Valladolid's main plaza then follow Calle 41 west for two blocks, where it forks. Go left (Calle 41a) for another three blocks.

In front of you stands the bright yellow San Bernardino de Siena, a 16th-century Franciscan church and monastery. Often targeted by indigenous rebellions, the interior is practically bare.

Nohoch Mul, the tallest pyramid in the northern Yucatán peninsula

Continue southwest a few blocks to the Cenote Dzitnup, signposted on the outkirts.

Have a refreshing dip in this beautiful *cenote* before returning to the main plaza. Park, visit the church of San Servacio, shop, then have lunch.

Drive back 28km along Highway 180 to Chemax and take a turn-off to the right to Cobá. Another 30km brings you to this striking archaeological site in the jungle (▶ 86). Leave Cobá by following signs to Tulum, then watch for a turn-off to the left after a few kilometres. This brings you to Tres Reyes and back to Highway 180 or the toll road to Cancún.

Where To...

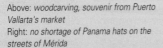

Above: *woodcarving, souvenir from Puerto Vallarta's market*
Right: *no shortage of Panama hats on the streets of Mérida*

Central Mexico

Price Categories

Restaurants are categorised as follows per person, including a beer or aperitif:

£ = up to $100 (pesos)
££ = $100–150 (pesos)
£££ = $150–250 (pesos)

Chiles en Nogada

This traditional Pueblan dish was once only available during the autumn pomegranate season, but deep-freezes have changed this. It consists of a gloriously creamy sauce of ground almonds and milk sprinkled with pomegranate seeds, coating a stuffed green pepper. At the heart of the dish is a complex stuffing of minced beef and veal, raisins, almonds and pine-nuts, all bound with egg. When it's good, it's very, very good!

Mexico City

Auseba (££)

The Zona Rosa's traditional favourite for people-watching with tea or coffee and delicious cakes – try the *mousse au chocolat*.

✉ Hamburgo 159B, Zona Rosa
☎ 511 3770 🕐 Daily,
9AM–10:30PM, Sun from 11AM
🚇 Insurgentes

Bar l'Opéra (££)

Sumptuously ornate *belle époque* decoration in this Parisian look-alike watering-hole. A favourite with artists and literati for evening drinks, but the food is mediocre.

✉ 5 de Mayo 10, Centro
☎ 512 8959 🕐 Daily 7PM–1AM
🚇 Bellas Artes

Café del Palacio (££)

Choose between a sunny terrace overlooking Alameda Park or a superb art deco interior. The short but varied menu includes large, hygenically prepared salads and international dishes.

✉ Palacio de Bellas Artes, Avenida Juárez, Centro ☎ 512 0807 🕐 Tue–Sun 10–8, until 1AM after performances
🚇 Bellas Artes

Caffé Milano (££)

An established Zona Rosa favourite for authentic Italian cuisine: pasta, fish and meat dishes. Outdoor tables or coolly designed interior.

✉ Amberes 27 ☎ 207 0119
🕐 Daily 8AM–2AM
🚇 Insurgentes

Cicero (£££)

Refined Mexican cuisine in a theatrical hacienda-style setting, with antiques and a cosy wood-panelled bar. This is the place to indulge to the full – try the plantains stuffed with ground beef as a starter. Live music means a cover charge.

✉ Londres 195, Zona Rosa
☎ 533 4276 🕐 Mon–Sat
1PM–1AM 🚇 Sevilla

Los Girasoles (££)

Colourful, elegant setting overlooking Plaza Tolsa. Exquisite Mexican *nouvelle cuisine* mostly inspired by pre-Hispanic recipes and ingredients. Try the chicken in tamarind *mole*. Good service, innovative *mariachis*, bar.

✉ Tacuba 8/10, Centro
☎ 510 0630 🕐 Mon–Sat
1PM–1AM, Sun 1–6PM 🚇 Bellas Artes

Hostería de Santo Domingo (£)

Claims to be Mexico City's oldest restaurant. Graffiti liberally adorns the walls between old photos and pictures. The speciality is *chiles en nogada* all year round. Reasonable quality, erratic but friendly service.

✉ Belisario Domínguez 72, Centro ☎ 526 5276 🕐 Daily 10AM–10:30PM 🚇 Allende

Madero (£)

Popular local restaurant buzzing with afternoon activity. Good-value set menus served 2–5PM. Useful stop-over location between Zócalo and Bellas Artes.

✉ Francisco Madero 36, Centro ☎ 510 2761 🕐 Lunch, dinner daily until 9:30
🚇 Allende

San Angel Inn (£££)

The place to lunch or dine in elegant San Angel. A superb 18th-century hacienda with gardens and patio. Award-winning international cuisine. Booking essential, but the patio also functions as a relaxing bar.

✉ **Diego Rivera 50, corner Altavista, San Angel** ☎ **616 1402** 🕐 **Mon–Sat 1PM–1AM, Sun 1–10PM**

Sanborns (£)

Spectacular atrium restaurant in the historic Casa de los Azulejos (House of Tiles). Digest afterwards looking at Orozco's 1925 mural, 'Omniscience' or shop in the same establishment.

✉ **Francisco Madero 4, Centro** ☎ **512 2233/1331** 🕐 **Daily 7AM–1AM** 🚇 **San Juan de Letrán**

Guadalajara
El Abajeño (££)

A Guadalajaran landmark with top *mariachis* thrown in. Attractive courtyard dining and bar, Jaliscan specialities, friendly service.

✉ **Avenida Vallarta 2802, Minerva** ☎ **630 0307** 🕐 **Lunch and dinner**

La Destilería (££)

Combined restaurant and tequila museum with unmistakably Mexican décor and menu. Over 80 varieties of tequila (which originated in this state) are on offer.

✉ **Avenida México 2916** ☎ **640 3110** 🕐 **Mon–Sat 1PM–midnight, Sun 1–6PM**

Guanajuato
Real de la Esperanza (££)

Converted chapel set high above the town offering sweeping views, sophisticated cuisine and an outdoor bar area. Good beef and pork dishes, salads.

✉ **Carretera Guanajuato-Dolores Hidalgo Km 5,**

Valenciana ☎ **(473) 21041** 🕐 **From 1PM**

Tasca de los Santos (£)

In a great location opposite Basílica to catch morning sun. Large breakfasts; paella is the speciality for later.

✉ **Plaza de la Paz 28** ☎ **(473) 22320** 🕐 **Daily 9AM–1AM**

El Truco (£)

An atmospheric, arty café/bar/ restaurant tucked down a side-street beside the Basílica. Good-value set menus. Lively background music.

✉ **Calle del Truco 7** ☎ **(473) 28374** 🕐 **Daily 9AM–midnight**

Querétaro
El Meson de Chico El Rota (£)

One of several terrace restaurants on the main square. Excellent Caesar salad and *nopalitos con queso*. Meat and seafood dishes.

✉ **Pasteur Sur 16, Centro** ☎ **(42)124295** 🕐 **Daily for breakfast, lunch, dinner**

Meson de Santa Rosa (££)

Stunning 300-year-old mansion hotel with romantic courtyard dining. Not to be missed, if only for a drink. Excellent, friendly service.

✉ **Pasteur 17 Sur** ☎ **(42) 242623** 🕐 **Lunch and dinner**

San Miguel del Allende
Restaurante Bella Italia (£)

Top-notch Italian cuisine. Freshly made pasta and salads in courtyard garden beside Bellas Artes. Good service and value.

✉ **Hernández Macías 50** ☎ **(415) 24989** 🕐 **Lunch and dinner**

Mole

This is not some form of Mexican donkey but one of the country's most popular sauces used on chicken or turkey. Although the name is Náhuatl (the language of the Aztecs), legend has it that it was invented in a Pueblan convent by a group of nuns desperate to disguise the flavour of a rather scrawny turkey for the visit of a Viceroy. Into a basic chocolate sauce went numerous spices, herbs, chillies, cinnamon and almonds, which was then simmered slowly for three days. Today, although the *mole* specialists are the towns of Puebla and Oaxaca, the dish is widely available throughout the country and the sauce can be bought in the markets.

The North & Baja California

Cocktails and Margaritas

The term 'cocktail' is said to have originated in Mexico when British naval crews stopping in Campeche started mixing their rum with other ingredients. When mixing spoons ran out one day, an ingenious waiter introduced the root of a plant known as the 'tail of a cock'. By the 1920s cocktails, had become the rage in Europe and the USA. Queen of this menu is the margarita, said to have originated in Chihuahua. The ingredients are white tequila, Triple Sec (or Cointreau), limes, crushed ice and salt. In coastal resorts this is often served frozen.

Los Cabos

Da Giorgio (££–£££)
Acclaimed Italian restaurant in spectacular clifftop site. Home-made pasta, scampi, pizzas, seafood. Live music during season. New branch opened at Misiones del Cabo, overlooking El Arco.
⌧ **Highway 1, 4km from San José del Cabo** ☎ **(114) 21988/33988** 🕐 1–11PM

Damiana (££)
Colourful, romantic restaurant with patio dining at the heart of San José. Sophisticated cuisine includes char-broiled lobster and jumbo prawns.
⌧ **Paseo Mijares 8, San José del Cabo** ☎ **(114) 20499 (reservation recommended)** 🕐 Daily 10:30AM–10:30PM

Mama Mia (£)
Popular, relaxed restaurant. International dishes, seafood, live music, fun atmosphere.
⌧ **Km 29.5 Carretera Transpeninsular, San José del Cabo** ☎ **(114) 23940** 🕐 Breakfast, lunch and dinner

Panchos (£)
Colourful Mexican restaurant offering hearty traditional dishes and seafood. Tortilla soup, *chile relleno* and lobster specialities. Live music nightly.
⌧ **Calle Hidalgo Corner Zapata, Cabo San Lucas** ☎ **(114) 30973** 🕐 6AM–11PM

Chihuahua

Chihuahua Charlie's (£)
A popular branch of the Anderson's chain of restaurants serving a wide choice of meat dishes and salads. Cheerful service and setting.
⌧ **Avenida Juárez 3329** ☎ **(14) 157065**

Ensenada

El Rey Sol (£££)
Award-winning restaurant serving French Provençal and Mexican dishes. Elegant, colonial-style setting.
⌧ **Avenida López Mateos 1000** ☎ **(617) 81733** 🕐 Lunch and dinner

Guerrero Negro

Malarrimo (£–££)
Delicious seafood including abalone, shrimp and fish. Ask here about natural history and cave-painting tours.
⌧ **Boulevard Emiliano Zapata (near entrance to town)** ☎ **(115) 70250**

Loreto

Café Olé (£)
Popular US-style restaurant. Steaks, salads and seafood; cheerful atmosphere.
⌧ **Madero** ☎ **(113) 50496**

Cesar's (££)
Acclaimed seafood in a well-established restaurant. Large portions of red snapper, lobster and other fresh produce. Friendly service.
⌧ **Emiliano Zapata, corner Benito Juárez** ☎ **(113) 30203** 🕐 Lunch and dinner

La Paz

El Moro (£)
Beachfront restaurant on road towards Pichilingue peninsula. Wide choice, including seafood, salads.
⌧ **Carretera Pichilingue Km 2.5** ☎ **(112) 27010** 🕐 Tue–Sat 8AM–10PM

Terraza del Perla (£)
Open-air restaurant of an established seafront hotel. Popular for large breakfasts and great snacks at any time.
⌧ **Alvaro Obregón 1570** ☎ **(112) 20777**

Pacific Mexico

Acapulco

Beto's Condesa (££)
A popular beachside restaurant. Seafood includes lobster and shrimp specialities, also Mexican and steak dishes. Live music and great views.

⊠ **Playa Condesa, Costera Miguel Alemán** ☎ **(74) 840473** ⏲ **Noon–midnight**

Carlos 'n Charlie's (£–££)
This well-known resort chain serves decent food at reasonable prices. Lively atmosphere, loud rock music and fast service.

⊠ **Costera Miguel Alemán 112, near the El Presidente Hotel** ☎ **(74) 840039** ⏲ **6PM–late**

Coyuca 22 (£££)
Unique hilltop setting with fabulous bay views. Superlative international cuisine, professional service. Elegant dress required. Booking essential.

⊠ **Carretera Las Brisas** ☎ **(74) 835030** ⏲ **Nov–Apr only**

Raffaello (£–££)
Branch of a popular Mexico City Italian restaurant. Home-made pasta, Caesar salad, fresh oysters and seafood dishes. Friendly service.

⊠ **Costera Miguel Alemán 1221** ☎ **(74) 840100** ⏲ **Dec–Apr, Jul, Aug**

Mazatlán

Doney (£)
Reasonably priced local restaurant, popular for extended lunches. Traditional Mexican dishes, seafood, steaks. Attractive décor includes old local photos.

⊠ **Mariano Escobedo 610, corner Cinco de Mayo** ☎ **(69) 812651** ⏲ **8AM–10:30PM**

El Parador Español (£–££)
Spanish cuisine and seafood specialities. Popular, lively place with good service.

⊠ **Avenida Camarón Sábalo, next to El Cid** ☎ **(69) 130767** ⏲ **7AM–midnight**

El Patio (££)
Good lobster, steak and Mexican dishes; extensive wine list. Comfortable, rustic setting with outdoor eating and live music in evenings.

⊠ **Avenida del Mar 30** ☎ **(69) 817301** ⏲ **8AM–2AM**

El Shrimp Bucket (£)
More fun in the evening when live *marimba* music enlivens the atmosphere. Mainly seafood; outdoor dining, great sea views.

⊠ **Olas Altas 11** ☎ **(69) 828019** ⏲ **6AM–11PM**

Puerto Vallarta

Archie's Wok (££)
Delicious Thai and Chinese specialities include garlic shrimp, Changmai fish and numerous vegetarian dishes.

⊠ **Francisca Rodríguez 130, near Playa Los Muertos** ☎ **(322) 20411** ⏲ **2–11PM. Closed Sun**

La Palapa (££)
Vallarta's original beachfront restaurant. Excellent seafood menu. Great position and ambience, candle-lit dinners.

⊠ **Calle Pulpito on Playa Los Muertos** ☎ **(322) 25225** ⏲ **Daily 8AM–11PM**

Red Cabbage Café (£–££)
Unusual décor plastered with photos of art, film and literary heroes and heroines. Friendly atmosphere and imaginative dishes.

⊠ **Riviera del Rio 204A** ☎ **(322) 30411** ⏲ **5–11PM**

Seafood
With nearly 10,000km of coastline in Mexico, it's not surprising that seafood features prominently on every menu. *Ceviche*, a popular starter, is made of chopped raw fish marinated in lime juice and further flavoured with chopped chilli and tomato. This can be delicious but should only be eaten in reputable restaurants. *Camarones* (shrimps) are another favourite, often simply grilled and served with a squeeze of lime or, *al mojo de ajo* (fried in garlic).

The South

From Iguanas to Flowers

Oaxaca is one of the states where culinary imagination takes off. If you are not sampling iguana (served in a stew and with a taste and texture resembling chicken), it may be one of the many Oaxacan variations on the squash theme. Courgette flowers are a great delicacy, while young squash vines are made into a popular soup. A relative of the squash is the *chayote*, a pear-shaped vegetable grown on a vine that comes into its own, when combined with garlic, tomato or chilli.

Huatulco

Café Huatulco (£)

The place to go when you want a decent coffee. Pretty kiosk in leafy main square that serves real espresso and other coffee specialities. Coffee beans come straight from the hills behind.

✉ **Kiosko de Santa Cruz, Plaza Principal, Santa Cruz** ☎ (958) 70339 ◷ 9:30AM–11PM

Oasis Café (£)

A popular spot on the main square. Seafood, grilled meats, salads, sushi. Dine inside or out.

✉ **Bugambilla, corner Flamboyant, La Crucecita** ☎ (958) 70045 ◷ 7AM–midnight

Tipsy's Restaurant (£)

Large beachfront restaurant with tables under *palapas*. Specialises in grilled meats, shellfish and fish. Try a lobster or prawn *taco*.

✉ **Bahía de Santa Cruz, behind Capitania de Puerto** ☎ (958) 70576 ◷ 11AM–11PM

Oaxaca

Café del Instituto de Artes Gráficas (£)

Oaxaca's most peaceful patio for a shady, light, cheap lunch. Oaxacan specialities (*tortas*, *tostadas*), fresh juices, coffee with mint.

✉ **Alcala 507** ☎ (951) 66980 ◷ Breakfast, lunch till 7:30PM

Del Vitral (££)

Elegant mansion setting just two blocks from zócalo. Sophisticated, international cuisine, Oaxacan specialities.

✉ **Guerrero 201** ☎ (951) 63124 ◷ Daily 12:30–11PM

Los Patos (££)

Romantic patio restaurant; the upper terrace has close-up views of Santo Domingo. Oaxacan specialities, full bar; contemporary paintings from adjoining art gallery.

✉ **Constitución 104** ☎ (951) 61704 ◷ 1PM–11PM

El Topil (££)

Family-run restaurant serving hearty Oaxacan meat dishes and delicious soups. Friendly atmosphere, though service can be slow.

✉ **Plazuela Labastida 104** ☎ (951) 41617 ◷ 7:30PM–11PM

Puerto Ángel

Restaurant Susy (£)

Pleasant beachfront spot with tables under shady *palapas*. Ultra-fresh lobster, oysters, fish and *ceviche*, as well as generous fruit salads.

✉ **Playa del Panteon** ☎ (958) 43019

San Cristóbal

Café La Selva (£)

Elegant coffee-house in contemporary style. Excellent coffee in all forms, snacks, cakes; newspapers.

✉ **Avenida Cresencio Rosas, corner Cuauhtémoc** ☎ (967) 87243

Veracruz

Gran Café del Portal (£)

Stunning old coffee house and restaurant, once known as La Parroquía. Still has its original 1810 period décor.

✉ **Independencia, corner Zamora** ☎ (29) 312759 ◷ Daily 6AM–midnight

La Fuente de Mariscos (££)

A wide variety of fresh seafood from the Atlantic. Live rock and salsa bands.

✉ **Hernán Cortés 1524** ☎ (29) 382412 ◷ Long lunches only

The Yucatán Peninsula

Campeche

Casa Vieja (££)

Overlooks the main square from the balcony. Varied menu, funky interior, bright colours, bar and music.

 Calle 10 No 319, between 55 and 57 ☎ (981) 15529

Cancún

Los Almendros (££)

Classic Yucatecan fare such as *poc chuc* and *cochinita pibil*. Live trio music in evening. In downtown area.

⊠ Avenida Bonampak, corner Avenida Sayil ☎ (98) 871332 🕒 10:30AM–11PM

Captain's Cove (££)

Palapa restaurant overlooking lagoon. Ultra-fresh seafood specialities, barbecued meats and Mexican dishes. Happy hour 4–7PM.

⊠ Boulevard Kukulcán, Km 9.5 ☎ (98) 850016 🕒 Daily 7AM–11PM

La Dolce Vita (£££)

Excellent Italian cuisine: fresh pasta, seafood, salads. Attentive service. Booking advisable.

⊠ Boulevard Kukulcán, Km 14.6, opposite Hotel Marriott ☎ (98) 850150 🕒 Lunch and dinner

Cozumel

Gallito Sol (££)

Interestingly designed restaurant with outdoor dining. *Nouvelle cuisine*, meat, seafood, salads, soups.

⊠ Avenida 5 Sur No 148, on Plaza Principal ☎ (987) 25238

Lobster's Cove (££–£££)

Up-market restaurant on seafront, south of main square. Lobster, pasta, seafood and flambéed desserts. Live music in the evenings.

⊠ Avenida Rafael Melgar 790, between Calle 9 and 11 Sur ☎ (987) 24022 🕒 Daily noon–11PM

Isla Mujeres

Zazil-Ha (££)

Romantic outdoor setting in hotel garden. Wide-ranging menu includes salads, seafood, pasta and meat dishes. Good bar with 7–9PM happy hour.

⊠ Playa Norte ☎ (987) 70279 🕒 Daily 7:30AM–10PM

Mérida

Los Almendros (££)

Famous Yucatecan restaurant. Fine choice of local specialities; regional show on Fridays at 7.

⊠ Calle 50-A No 493, Plaza de la Mejorada ☎ (99) 285459 🕒 Daily 9AM–11PM

La Bella Epoca (£)

Delightful *fin de siècle* interior with balconies overlooking the square. International, vegetarian and Yucatecan dishes. Attentive service; downstairs bar.

⊠ Parque Hidalgo, Calle 60 No 497 ☎ (99) 281429 🕒 11AM–midnight

Playa del Carmen

Blue Lobster (££)

Palapa-roofed restaurant with sea views. Lobster, seafood, pasta, meat dishes and flambéed desserts.

⊠ Avenida 5, between Calle 4 and 6 ☎ (987) 31360 🕒 7AM–11PM

La Parilla (£–££)

Established, popular restaurant on Playa's main drag. Salads, seafood, Mexican dishes.

⊠ Avenida 5, corner Calle 8 ☎ (987) 30687 🕒 7AM–1AM

Yucatecan Cuisine

Unique in Mexico due to its prolonged isolation, Yucatecan cuisine combines influences from Europe (particularly France), New Orleans and Cuba. Common dishes include *sopa de lima*, a delicious chicken broth of shredded chicken, *tortilla* and lime juice; *pollo* or *cochinita pibil*, chicken or pork marinaded in spices and sour orange juice then baked in banana leaves; and *poc chuc*, pork fillet marinated in sour orange juice and served with pickled onions. Another popular ingredient is *pavo*, wild turkey, which can be shredded, wrapped in *tortillas*, pickled or stewed in soups.

97

Central Mexico

Price-Categories

Approximate price for a double room with attached shower or bathroom per night:

£ = $120 – 250 (pesos)
££ = $250 – 600 (pesos)
£££ = $600 (pesos) upwards

In beach resorts, walk-in prices rocket in high season (Dec–Apr), so add on about 30 per cent to the above categories.

Mexico City

Hotel Canada (££)

A centrally located, modern hotel. Reasonable rates and spacious, clean rooms. Air-conditioning, restaurant, parking.

✉ **Cinco de Mayo 47, Centro**
☎ **(5) 518 2106, fax: 512 9310**
Ⓜ **Allende**

Hotel de Cortés (££)

Legendary hotel in former 18th-century hospice. Large courtyard restaurant; can be noisy but in a convenient location.

✉ **Hidalgo 85, Centro**
☎ **(5) 518 2181, fax: 512 1863**
Ⓜ **Hidalgo**

Hotel Gillow (£)

Large hotel in heart of the historic centre. The interior lacks charm but rooms are comfortable and good value.

✉ **Isabel La Católica 17, Centro** ☎ **(5) 518 1440/6**
Ⓜ **Allende**

Hotel Majestic (££)

Plum location overlooking Zócalo. Colonial-style décor, terrace restaurant. Part of Best Western group.

✉ **Madero 73, Centro**
☎ **(5) 521 8600, fax: 512 6262**
Ⓜ **Zócalo**

Hotel Maria Cristina (££)

Charming colonial hotel with gardens, patio, piano bar, restaurant and plenty of atmosphere. Book ahead. Just north of Zona Rosa.

✉ **Río Lerma 31** ☎ **(5) 703 1787** Ⓜ **Insurgentes**

Vasco de Quiroga (££)

Friendly family hotel on quieter, eastern side of Zona Rosa. Fifty well-furnished, colonial-style rooms. Restaurant.

✉ **Londres 15, Zona Rosa**
☎ **(5) 546 2614, fax: 535 2257**
Ⓜ **Insurgentes**

Cuernavaca

Hotel Bajo El Volcán (££)

Well-appointed, central hotel whose name refers to Malcolm Lowry's book. Parking, pool, bar, restaurant.

✉ **Alejandro de Humboldt**
☎ **(73) 124873**

Hotel Las Hortensias (£)

In a very central location with modest but clean and adequate rooms opening on to pretty garden courtyard.

✉ **Hidalgo 22** ☎ **(73) 185265, fax: 123061**

Guadalajara

Hotel Frances (££)

Popular, historic old hotel close to Plaza de la Liberación. Inside patio, restaurant, bar, antiques. Comfortable modernised rooms.

✉ **Maestranza 35** ☎ **(3) 613 1190**

Plaza Génova (£)

Well-located modern hotel. Good value, comfortable rooms; clean.

✉ **Avenida Juárez 123**
☎ **(3) 613 7500, fax: 614 8253**

Guanajuato

Hotel San Diego (££)

Popular hotel overlooking the main square. Reasonable rooms, restaurant.

✉ **Jardín de la Unión 1**
☎ **(473) 21300, fax: 25626**

Posada Santa Fé (£££)

Elegant mansion with antique furnishings and well-appointed rooms. Excellent restaurant with outside tables on main square. Parking.

✉ **Plaza Principal 12** ☎ **(473) 20084, fax: 24653**

Jalapa

Posada del Cafeto (£)

Attractively decorated little hotel down a peaceful side street. Cheerful, fresh rooms but rather surly service.

✉ Canovas 12 ☎ (28) 170023

Morelia

Hotel Casino (££)

Reasonably priced hotel overlooking main square and cathedral. Colonial style, good amenities, popular outdoor café under arches.

✉ Portal Hidalgo 229 ☎ (43) 131053/101

Pátzcuaro

Hotel Los Escudos (£)

Elegant hotel on scenic main square. Well-appointed rooms surround leafy patios. Popular restaurant. Parking.

✉ Portal Hidalgo 73 ☎ (434) 20138/21290

Puebla

Hotel Colonial (£–££)

Modernised colonial hotel on main square. Small but reasonable rooms.

✉ Calle 4 Sur 105 ☎ (22) 464612, fax: 460818

Posada Linda (£–££)

Canadian-owned patio hotel close to centre. Some suites with kitchenettes.

✉ Calle 7 Sur 303 ☎ (22) 322462

Querétaro

Hotel Impala (££)

Modern hotel overlooking Parque Alameda. Decent rooms but front ones are noisy. Restaurant, parking.

✉ Colón 1, Centro ☎ (42) 122570, fax: 124515

Hotel Mesón de Santa Rosa (££)

Very attractive colonial-style hotel on main square with excellent patio restaurant. Upper end of price category, but good value.

✉ Pasteur Sur 17, Centro ☎ (42) 242623, fax: 125522

La Casa de la Marquesa (£££)

One of Querétaro's most beautiful mansions. Luxurious, individually decorated suites, exotically furnished with antiques. Part of 'small luxury hotels of the world' group.

✉ Madero 41, Centro ☎ (42) 120092, fax: 120098

San Miguel del Allende

Hotel Posada de San Francisco (££)

Excellent colonial-style hotel. Small but well-furnished rooms with heating. Restaurant in front courtyard.

✉ Plaza Principal 2 ☎ (415) 20072

Mansion Virreyes (££)

Small but nicely furnished rooms surrounding a courtyard. Good restaurant. Rates include breakfast.

✉ Canal 19 ☎ (415) 23355

Posada de las Monjas (£–££)

Converted monastery with comfortable rooms in a peaceful but central location. Friendly and popular. Restaurant, parking.

✉ Calle Canal 37 ☎ (415) 20171, fax: 26227

Taxco

Hotel Agua Escondida (£)

Well situated; rooms on the main square with terrace views of the cathedral. Rooftop pool, good children's facilities, parking.

✉ Plaza Borda 4 ☎ (762) 21166

Hotel Posada San Javier (£)

Excellent value 19-room hotel surrounding palm-shaded garden in central location. Rustic furnishings, balconies. Small pool, garage.

✉ Ex-Rastro 4, Estacas 1 ☎ (762) 202231 fax: (819) 22351

Colonial Hotels

Central Mexico is the best area to experience the atmosphere of converted colonial mansions or haciendas. The latter are often outside town and high-priced, so not always suitable, but many of the former are very affordable. On top of this, their historic background puts them in the heart of town and, at best, on the zócalo or main square. Check rooms before registering to ensure the noise level is not too high.

The North & Baja California

Margarita

For once this is not a reference to Mexico's favourite cocktail but the name of a dynamic guest-house owner in Creel, along the Copper Canyon route. For years backpackers were hauled off the Chihuahua–Pacifico train to stay at her expansive and friendly guest house, indulging in generous communal meals before being whisked around the canyons by members of her extended family. Today, her operation has expanded considerably and no traveller will find themselves without a bed for the night.

Barranca del Cobre (Copper Canyon)
Hotel Divisadero Barrancas (£–££)
Spectacularly sited, looking over Urique canyon. Good rooms with satellite TV, restaurant, bar, parking.
✉ **Divisadero Barrancas Km 622, Urique** ☎ **(14) 151199/156575**

Los Cabos
Hotel Posada Real Los Cabos (££)
Low-rise hotel in beautiful cactus garden leading to beach. Comfortable air-conditioned rooms, pool, tennis, sport fishing facilities.
✉ **Malecón San José, Zona Hotelera, San José del Cabo** ☎ **(114) 20155/20636**

Chihuahua
Hotel San Francisco (££)
Modern hotel behind the cathedral. Amenities include bar, restaurant, travel desk.
✉ **Victoria 409** ☎ **(14) 167770**

Ensenada
El Cid Hotel (££)
Small-scale, Best Western hotel close to the bay. Strong accent on Mexican décor. Restaurant, bar, parking.
✉ **Avenida López Mateos 993** ☎ **(617) 82401**

Loreto
Hotel Mision de Loreto (£)
Attractively designed hotel overlooking sea. Spacious rooms with air-conditioning. Large pool, bar, parking.
✉ **Boulevard López Mateos 1** ☎ **(113) 50048**

Hotel La Pinta (££)
Good standard air-conditioned rooms with satellite TV. Attractive pool with *palapas* and sea view; restaurant, bar, parking.
✉ **Calle Francisco Madero, Playa Loreto** ☎ **(113) 50025/50600**

Mulegé
Vista Hermosa (££)
Comfortable holiday suites with views over estuary. Facilities include a pool, airstrip, boats and guides.
✉ **Camino al Puerto** ☎ **(115) 30222**

La Paz
Hotel Club El Moro (£)
Pleasant, friendly hotel across road from sea; air-conditioned rooms with satellite TV and balconies surrounding small pool.
✉ **Carretera Pichilingue Km 2, Colonia Colina del Sol** ☎ **(112) 24084**

La Posada de Engelbert (££)
Nicely designed, low-rise beachfront hotel in lovely gardens. Spacious rooms and villas with air-conditioning and satellite TV. Restaurant, bar with live music.
✉ **Nueva Reforma, corner Playa Sur** ☎ **(112) 24011/20663**

San Felipe
Hotel Las Misiones San Felipe (££)
Modern hotel with some good views. Comfortable rooms. Pool, bar, parking.
✉ **Avenida Misión Loreto 148, Playa San Felipe** ☎ **(657) 71280**

San Ignacio
Posada San Ignacio (£)
Good-value, friendly hotel with comfortable rooms. Organises cave-painting and whale-watching tours.
✉ **Avenida Venustiano Carranza 2** ☎ **(115) 40313**

Pacific Mexico

Acapulco

Hotel Elcano Royal (£££)
Opposite golf course at eastern end of Costera, with pool overlooking beach. Well-appointed, spacious rooms, excellent restaurant, bars, good service.
✉ **Avenida Costera Miguel Alemán** ☎ **(74) 841950/1**

Hotel Los Flamingos (£)
Tranquil mid 1930s hotel once frequented by Cary Grant and Errol Flynn. Lovely garden, pool, air-conditioned rooms, good restaurant, parking, tour desk.
✉ **Avenida Adolfo López Mateos, Las Playas** ☎ **(74) 820690/1**

Ixtapa-Zihuatanejo

Hotel Fiesta Mexicana (££)
Beside the palm-fringed beach of La Ropa, a comfortable hotel with pool, tennis, coffee shop and tour desk.
✉ **Playa La Ropa, Zihuatanejo** ☎ **(755) 43776**

Hotel Irma (££)
Comfortable, well-run hotel with air-conditioned rooms high on the hillside overlooking the beach. Tennis, pool, coffee shop, tours.
✉ **La Madera, Playa La Madera, Zihuatanejo** ☎ **(755) 42105**

Hotel Posada Real (££)
Good family-style seafront hotel with air-conditioned rooms, pool, children's playground, tennis, restaurant, bar, boat tours.
✉ **Boulevard Ixtapa, Ixtapa** ☎ **(755) 31625**

Mazatlán

Hotel Azteca Inn (££)
Friendly hotel. Well-furnished rooms with satellite TV, some overlooking pool. Bar, coffee shop, parking.
✉ **Rodolfo T Loalza 307** ☎ **(69) 134477**

Hotel Costa de Oro (££)
Oceanside hotel with rooms arranged around inner patios, gardens, pool and open-air restaurant. Tennis, tours.
✉ **Camarón Sábalo, Zona Dorada** ☎ **(69) 135113**

Puerto Vallarta

Hotel Eloisa (££)
Well placed with air-conditioned rooms in the Olas Altas area of old Vallarta, behind Playa Los Muertos. Small pool, restaurant.
✉ **Lázaro Cárdenas 179** ☎ **(322) 26465**

Hotel Los Quatro Vientos (££)
A landmark 16-room hotel that saw all the movie stars. Lovely, breezy spot with great views from rooftop bar. Friendly, well-run.
✉ **Matamoros 520** ☎ **(322) 20161**

Hotel Rosita (££)
Vallarta's first hotel, overlooking main town beach, with clean, simple rooms. Good value for location.
✉ **Paseo Díaz Ordáz 901** ☎ **(322) 21351**

San Blas

Hotel Garza Canela (££)
Attractively designed hotel with gardens, pool, excellent restaurant. Comfortable, spacious rooms. Close to beach; birdwatching tours arranged.
✉ **Paredes Sur 106, Centro** ☎ **(328) 50112**

Last Resort Deals
If you are travelling in Mexico and want to stay in a beach resort such as Los Cabos, Puerto Vallarta or the Copper Canyon, some of the best deals on offer are with the regional airlines such as Aerocalifornia or Mexicana. Check out their flight and hotel offers at any travel agent: they are often cheaper than the return flight itself.

The South

Village Accommodation

A recent initiative set into motion by the state of Oaxaca offers an interesting budget alternative to Oaxaca's colonial-style hotels. Launched under the name of Tourist Yu'u is a string of eight purpose-built huts located in villages along the road between the state capital and Mitla. Each one contains four bunk beds, a kitchen and shower room, and is managed by a local villager. These make ideal self-catering bases for families or students, although their location makes hiring a car essential. Contact Sedetur (state tourist office) in Oaxaca for further information ☎ 951 60984, fax: 61500.

Huatulco
Hotel Marlin (££)
Pleasantly sized French-owned hotel, a few minutes' walk from the beach. Spacious air-conditioned rooms, restaurant, pool, travel desk. Efficiently run.
✉ **Paseo Mitla 107, Bahía de Santa Cruz** ☎ **(958) 70055**

Suites Begonias (£)
Central hotel at the heart of La Crucecita. Restaurant, room service.
✉ **Plaza Principal, La Crucecita** ☎ **(958) 70018**

Oaxaca
Casa Oaxaca (£££)
Superb new hotel, decorated with exceptional contemporary Mexican taste. Spacious rooms and patios, pool, paintings. Breakfast included in very reasonable rates.
✉ **García Vigil 407** ☎ **(951) 44173, fax: 64412**

Hostal La Noria (££–£££)
Tastefully decorated patio hotel in central location. Excellent restaurant and service. Singles, doubles or suites.
✉ **Hidalgo 918** ☎ **(951) 47844, fax: 63992**

Hotel Francia (£)
Large 46-room hotel, one block east of the zócalo. Spacious, clean rooms, friendly staff. Can be noisy.
✉ **20 de Noviembre 212** ☎ **(951) 64811, fax: 64251**

Puerto Ángel
Buena Vista (£)
Best location in Puerto Ángel, on hillside behind port. Imaginatively designed, simple rooms, some with balconies and hammocks. Large dining terrace.

✉ **Aptdo Postal 48** ☎ **(958) 43104**

Villa Serena Florencia (£)
Excellent value, Mediterranean-style inn beside fishing beach. Simple rooms with fan and/or air-conditioning. Good restaurant and sun terrace. Friendly.
✉ **Virgilio Uribe** ☎ **(958) 43044**

San Cristóbal de las Casas
Hotel Flamboyant Español (££)
Elegant, colonial-style hotel with well-appointed rooms off flowery patio. Restaurant, bar, gym, solarium.
✉ **Calle 1 de Marzo 15**
☎ **(967) 80045, fax: 80514**

Tuxtla Gutiérrez
Gran Hotel Humberto (£–££)
Large, central 1950s hotel with original furnishings. Good rooms, friendly staff, restaurant.
✉ **Avenida Central Poniente 180** ☎ **(961) 22504**

Veracruz
Hotel El Faro (£)
Family-run hotel tucked away a few streets back from harbour. Simple rooms with TV and air-conditioning or fan.
✉ **16 de Septiembre 223**
☎ **(29) 316538**

Hotel Mocambo (££)
Well-established favourite on Mocambo beach, about 8km south of town. Decent-sized rooms, some overlooking garden and beach. Pool, tennis court, travel desk, coffee shop.
✉ **Calzada Rúiz Cortines 4000, Colonia Mocambo, Boca del Río** ☎ **(29) 220205/6**

The Yucatán Peninsula

Campeche
Hotel America (£)
Converted mansion near main square; good-value double rooms, fan, TV. Some rooms still awaiting renovation. Safe parking at nearby Hotel Ramada.

 Calle 10 No 252 ☎ (981) 64588

Cancún
Few Cancún hotels see walk-in customers. They are best booked on a package basis through a travel agent.

Chichén Itzá
Hotel Hacienda Chichén (£££)
Lovely 16th-century hacienda hotel wih modern air-conditioned cottage accommodation. Beautiful gardens, pool, restaurant.

☒ Chichén Itzá ☎ (99) 242150, toll-free: 1800 624 8451

Cozumel
Hotel Casa del Mar (££)
Rustic-style hotel south of San Miguel overlooking ocean with air-conditioned rooms, pool, wet bar, restaurant, gardens.

☒ Costera Sur, Km 4 ☎ (987) 21900

Sol Cabañas del Caribe (££)
Intimate, beachfront hotel with rooms and cabins. Bar, restaurant and good beach.

☒ Carretera Costera Norte, Km 5.1 ☎ (987) 20161

Isla Mujeres
Posada del Mar (££)
One of Isla's earliest hotels in large garden overlooking sea. Spacious air-conditioned rooms, bright exterior colours, large pool, bar, restaurant. Efficiently run. Central but quiet location.

☒ Avenida Rueda Medina 15A ☎ (987) 70044, fax: 70266

Mérida
Gran Hotel (££)
Fabulous 1902 hotel with elegant, spacious rooms. All open on to a veranda surrounding leafy inner patio. Friendly and good value. Restaurant, parking.

☒ Calle 60 No 496, Parque Cepada ☎ (99) 247730/247822

Hotel Casa del Balam (£££)
Stylish central hotel in modernised 19th-century building. Soundproofing, pool, colonial features, satellite TV, travel agency, parking.

☒ Calle 60 No 488 ☎ (99) 242150

Playa del Carmen
Blue Parrot Inn (££–£££)
Established, hip favourite on beachfront. Variety of rooms, bungalows and *palapa* huts. Popular bar with live music; massages, restaurant.

☒ Calle 12 Norte ☎ (987) 30083

Cabañas Bananas (£)
Friendly, central old hotel with garden cabins or rooms. All have fans.

☒ Avenida 5 Norte, corner Calle 6 ☎ (987) 30036

Tulum
Nohoch Tunich (££)
Bungalows and cabins on beach. Italian restaurant.

☒ Carretera Tulum-Boca Paila, Km 5 ☎ (987) 12092

Piedra Escondida (£££)
Luxury but small-scale beachfront hotel. Excellent French-run restaurant, snorkelling and diving tours.

☒ Carretera Tulum-Boca Paila, Km 5 ☎ (987) 12092

Split Personality
As far as accommodation is concerned, the Yucatán peninsula is neatly divided into two halves. To the east is the Cancún-Tulum Corridor, where walk-in prices match the popularity and services. To the west are relaxed towns with a life outside tourism such as Valladolid (► 90), Campeche (► 86) and even Mérida (► 84). These, together with smaller places near by, offer excellent value both for food and hotels.

Markets

Markets

Many large towns have weekly markets that often bring streams of local people into the plaza. If you have already visited a few crafts shops to get an idea of what is commonly available and you see something exceptional in a market, buy it! You may not see it again.

Bargaining is part of any transaction, but remember how impoverished most of these people are.

Central Mexico

Mexico City

Bazar Sábado

Up-market handicrafts bazaar in the southern San Ángel neighbourhood spills on to pavements. Few bargains in silver, ceramics, glass, clothing and textiles, but a lively atmosphere.

⌧ **Plaza San Jacinto 11, San Ángel** 🕐 **Sat only 10–7**
🚌 **San Ángel *pesero* bus down Insurgentes**

La Ciudadela

An open-air treasure trove of handicrafts from all over the country surrounds a central courtyard. Bargaining is essential.

⌧ **Mercado de las Artesanías, Plaza de la Ciudadela, Calle Balderas** 🕐 **Mon–Sat 11–6, Sun 11–2** Ⓜ **Juárez or Balderas**

Guanajuato

Mercado Hidalgo

Superb turn-of-the-century iron-and-glass market building in town centre with food market on ground floor and upstairs stalls selling baskets, embroidered clothes, pottery, shawls and more.

⌧ **Avenida Juárez**
🕐 **Mon–Sat 9–6**

Morelia

Casa de las Artesanías

A vast handicrafts emporium located in a former convent. Wide choice of Michoacán lacquerware, woodcarvings, pottery, copper and furniture. Small museum on premises. Shipping arranged. Market stalls in plaza outside.

⌧ **Ex-Convento de San Francisco, Plaza Valladolid**
☎ **(43) 22486/ 21248**
🕐 **Daily 9–8**

Puebla

Mercado La Victoria

Central market next to Santo Domingo church. Upper floor offers Pueblan food specialities and wide range of handicrafts from the region. Some up-market craft shops on ground level.

⌧ **Calle 5 de Mayo, between Avenida 8 and 6** 🕐 **Mon–Sat 10:30–8**

The South

Oaxaca

Mercado de Artesanías

Large crafts market southwest of the zócalo. Rugs, textiles, jewellery, painted wooden animals and ceramics dominate. Bargaining essential.

⌧ **Zaragoza, corner J P García**
🕐 **Daily 11–8**

San Cristóbal de las Casas

Mercado José Castillo Tielmans

The main indigenous market for surrounding villages. Fabulous crafts and ethnic variety.

⌧ **Avenida General Utrilla, corner Nicaragua** 🕐 **Daily 6–3 (except Sun)**

The Yucatán Peninsula

Mérida

Mercado Municipal de Artesanías

A sprawling crafts market in two separate buildings. Mayan embroidered dresses, lace, hammocks, shellware, Panama hats. Prices are exorbitant and demand hard bargaining.

⌧ **Calle 65 corner Calle 56, behind post office (*Correos*)**
🕐 **Daily 8AM–9PM**

Art & Antiques

Central Mexico

Mexico City
Plaza San Angel
Mexico City's largest antiques centre. Furniture, paintings, decorative arts, silver, bric-à-brac. Weekend market stalls bring the area alive; watch out for copies.
✉ **Plaza del Angel, Londres 161 and Hamburgo 150, Zona Rosa** 🕐 **Daily 10–8; antiques market Sat–Sun 10–4** 🚇 **Insurgentes**

Puebla
Casa Poblana
Attractively renovated building in heart of Puebla's antique district, near the Sunday antiques market of Plazuela de los Sapos. Contemporary home objects (glass, ceramics, wood) beside unusual antiques.
✉ **Calle 6 Sur 406** ☎ **(22) 326043**

San Miguel del Allende
Bazar Unicornio
Large courtyard with unusual selection of antiques, hand-painted ex-votos, crosses in embossed silver and other religious objects.
✉ **Hernández Macías 80** ☎ **(415) 21306**

Pacific Mexico

Puerto Vallarta
Galería Museo Huichol
Large gallery specialising in Huichol art and crafts, giving direct support to the crafts-people. Demonstrations.
✉ **Morelos 490** ☎ **(322) 32141**

Galería Uno
Contemporary art gallery in attractive converted house. Paintings, sculptures, graphics and posters by well-known Mexican artists.
✉ **Morelos 561** ☎ **(322) 20908** 🕐 **Mon–Sat 10–8**

Olinala Gallery
Well-displayed choice selection of fine indigenous art. Ritual masks, Huichol beadwork, lapidary work and other rare original pieces.
✉ **Lázaro Cárdenas 274** ☎ **(322) 24995** 🕐 **Mon–Sat 10–2, 5–9PM**

The South

Huatulco
Galerías Huatulco
Contemporary works (paintings and sculptures) by artists from Oaxaca, Morelos, Michoacán and Jalisco. Also sells interesting jewellery designs in gold and silver.
✉ **Hotel Sheraton, Tangolunda** ☎ **(958) 10080** 🕐 **Mon–Sat 9–1, 5–7, Sun 9–2**

Oaxaca
Galería Gráfica Soruco
Interesting selection of works on paper, and photos.
✉ **Plazuela Labastida 104C** ☎ **(951) 43938**

Galería Quetzalli
Large contemporary art gallery showing best of young Oaxacan artists. Combined with a bar-restaurant.
✉ **Constitución 104** ☎ **(951) 42606/40030**

La Mano Mágica
Long-established Oaxacan art gallery with regular exhibitions of contemporary artists and rug designs. Adjoining handicrafts store.
✉ **Alcalá 203** ☎ **(951) 64275**

Archaeological Artefacts
Remember that it is strictly prohibited to export any pre-Hispanic artefact from Mexico. Countless vendors, particularly on archaeological sites, attempt to fob off ready-made 'artefacts' as the real thing. Buy one if you like it, but only pay its real handicraft value. Large stores and museums sell the best-quality copies.

Handicrafts

Pottery and Ceramics
Mexican craftspeople make an extraordinary variety of pottery and ceramics. Pueblan Talavera has the most refined traditional patterns, Michoacán the most extraordinary shapes, San Bartolomé, in Oaxaca, a unique metallic black range and Dolores Hidalgo, near Guanajuato, colourful cheap designs. Beware of using the heavier ceramics fired at low temperatures for food, as they have a dangerously high lead content that is easily absorbed.

Central Mexico

Mexico City

Fonart
Three branches of this state-run handicrafts store promise top-quality goods. Carved wooden furniture, pottery, ceramics, glass, textiles, jewellery, basket-ware and plenty more. Shipping arranged, fixed prices. The largest choice is at Patriotismo branch.
✉ **Avenida Patriotismo 691, Mixcoac. Also at Avenida Juárez 89, Centro; Presidente Carranza 115, Coyoacán** ☎ **598 1666** 🕔 **Mon–Sat 10–7**
🚇 **Mixcoac (main branch)**

The Green Door
Well-established handicrafts store with reasonable prices for jewellery, pottery and pre-Hispanic reproductions. Shipping service. A favourite with local expatriates.
✉ **Cedro 8, Colonia Santa Maria** ☎ **546 8005** 🚇 **San Cosme** 🕔 **Mon–Fri 9–5, Sat 9–1:30. Closed Sun**

La Luna Descalza
Good selection and imaginative display of handicrafts from all over Mexico. Lots of decorative tinwork. Near Bazar Sábado.
✉ **Plaza San Jacinto 3, San Angel** ☎ **616 4617** 🚇 **'San Angel'** *pesero* **bus down Insurgentes**

Cuernavaca

Casillas Artesanías
Good selection of handmade furnishing items and handi-crafts from the states of Michoacán, Guanajuato, Jalisco, Puebla and Oaxaca.
✉ **San Diego 805, Colonia Vista Hermosa** ☎ **(73) 163598** 🕔 **Daily**

Cerámica Santa María
Demonstrates and sells handpainted pottery. New techniques and designs developed over nearly 40 years.
✉ **Zapata 900, Centro** ☎ **(73) 130670**

Guanajuato

Casa de Artesanía
Reasonable variety of crafts from central Mexico in store located by historic hacienda outside town.
✉ **Ex-Hacienda San Gabriel de Barrera, Marfil** ☎ **(473) 22408** 🕔 **Wed–Sun 10–5**

Fonart
Wide selection of Mexican handicrafts at this state-owned store. Fixed prices and top quality.
✉ **Casa del Conde de la Valenciana, Km 5** ☎ **01473 22550** 🕔 **Daily 10–6**

Puebla

Uriarte
Renowned workshop and outlet for traditional Talavera ceramics, founded in 1824. Exquisitely hand-painted pieces, but expensive. Short tours of workshops Mon–Sat at 10, 11, noon and 1PM.
✉ **Avenida 4 Poniente 911, between Calle 9 and 11** ☎ **(22) 321598** 🕔 **Mon–Sat 9–6:30, Sun 11–6**

Querétaro

Casa Queretana de Las Artesanías
Wide range of local craftwork and interior decoration items. Lace, bed and table linen, pottery, wooden furniture.
✉ **Andador Libertad 52, Centro** ☎ **(142) 141235** 🕔 **Daily**

Florería Encanto
Large store with good

selection of reasonably priced pottery from Dolores Hidalgo and glassware from Guadalajara.

✉ **Pasteur Sur 29** ☎ **(42) 123737**

Fonart

Dependable state-owned handicrafts shop with items from all over the country. Policy aims to give artisans better prices.

✉ **Angela Peralta 20, Centro** ☎ **(142) 122648**

San Miguel de Allende

Bazar Romero & Flores

Large shop opposite Instituto Allende with wide choice of metal lamps in copper, brass or perforated tin. Wrought-iron candle-holders, hand-blown glass.

✉ **Ancha de San Antonio 13** ☎ **(415) 27274**

Casa del Inquisidor

Historic house converted into labyrinthine arts, crafts and home furnishings shop.

✉ **Cuadrante 36** ☎ **(415) 21325**

Taxco

Fonart

The state-owned handicrafts chain strikes again. Reliable quality, though smaller selection at this branch.

✉ **Calle Juan Ruiz de Alarcón 8, Local 1001 Plaza Taxco** ☎ **01762 24818**

The North and Baja California

Los Cabos

Casa Mexicana

Wide selection of Mexican handicrafts from Talavera pottery to wooden furniture.

✉ **Main plaza, Avenida Cabo San Lucas, Cabo San Lucas** ☎ **(114) 31933** 🕐 **Daily 4–10PM**

Copal

Attractively converted old house with fine selection of handicrafts from all over Mexico. Taxco silver, hand-blown glass, rattan furniture, masks, rugs, pottery.

✉ **Plaza Mijares 10, San José del Cabo** ☎ **(114) 161296**

Pacific Mexico

Puerto Vallarta

Quetzalcóatl

Spacious emporium of indigenous art such as beaded Huichol pieces, black pottery from Oaxaca, Aztec and Maya reproductions, masks and terracotta sculptures. Shipping arranged.

✉ **Juárez 428** ☎ **(322) 32380** 🕐 **Mon–Sat 9:30–8:30**

Shapes

Interesting shop and work-shop making reproductions of Paquimé pottery in all shapes and sizes.

✉ **Aquíles Serdán 406** ☎ **(322) 23890**

The South

Oaxaca

La Casa de la Iguana

Lizards are the theme here, but sells many other unusual items from all over Mexico. Furniture and lamps too.

✉ **Allende 109** ☎ **(951) 60588**

Fruto del Telar

Wide selection of woollen rugs in Teotitlán del Valle style. Some innovative geometric designs.

✉ **Cinco de Mayo 400B** ☎ **(951) 61534**

Mujeres Artesanas de las Regiones de Oaxaca

Sprawling showroom/shop displaying craftswork by local women's co-operative. Pottery, woodcarvings, weaving, embroidered clothes, leatherwork and much more. Packaging.

✉ **Calle 5 de Mayo 204** ☎ **(951) 60670**

Siesta Time

When you are in southern Mexico and coastal resorts, forget about shopping in the afternoon. This is siesta or beach time. Most shops open around 9AM, then close at 1 or 2 for lunch, reopening at 4 or 5 and staying open until 8 or 9.

Clothing &
Accessories

Fashion Buys

If you are not taken by Westernised Mexican fashion, traditional clothes, shawls and textiles, buy something original. Intricately embroidered textiles from Oaxaca and Chiapas are now collector's items, but a *guayabera* (a loose-fitting man's shirt) from the Yucatán will not break the bank, nor will a handwoven *serape* (shawl), unless it is silk. Leather belts come in countless designs and are great bargains.

Central Mexico

Mexico City
Casa Cuesta
Good quality, ready-made men's clothing and tailoring in fabrics ranging from cashmere to silk. Not cheap.
⊠ **Rio Sena 87a, across Reforma from Zona Rosa** ☎ **208 1677** 🚇 **Cuauhtémoc**

Zara
Stylish clothes usually in synthetic blends, made in Spain and sometimes reasonably priced. Bags, shoes and accessories too.
⊠ **Madero 50, corner Isabel La Católica, Centro Histórico** ☎ **521 5900** 🚇 **Zócalo or Allende**

San Miguel de Allende
El Sombrero
Handmade straw and leather hats. Special orders made at San Francisco 30.
⊠ **San Francisco 14** ☎ **(415) 23675**

The North and Baja California

Los Cabos
La Sandia
Stylish women's clothes, accessories and jewellery inspired by pre-Hispanic designs.
⊠ **Plaza Mijares 6-B, San José del Cabo** ☎ **(114) 22230**

Pacific Mexico

Acapulco
Armando's
Light cotton women's jackets, dresses and other summerwear in clear, tropical colours, often finely embroidered.
⊠ **Costera Miguel Alemán 1252–7** ☎ **(74) 845111**

Esteban
Renowned local designer makes casual and evening wear for men and women to order. Ready-to-wear collection and accessories.
⊠ **Costera Miguel Alemán 2010** ☎ **(74) 843084**

Mazatlán
Gaby's Leather Factory
Understated-looking factory outlet offering good bargains in leather clothes and accessories for men and women. Made-to-measure within the day.
⊠ **Camarón Sábalo 1652** ☎ **(69) 161022**

The South

Huatulco
Ay Caramba! Kanoa Boutique
Casual sportswear and beach clothing.
⊠ **Hotel Flamboyant, Plaza Principal, La Crucecita** ☎ **(958) 70244**

Oaxaca
Dishvé
A change from Oaxaca's indigenous embroidered clothes. Cheesecloth and cotton women's wear, some accessories. See next door too.
⊠ **Plaza Santo Domingo, Alcalá 407** ☎ **(951) 42913**

The Yucatán Peninsula

Isla Mujeres
Qué Barbara
Unusual designs from Guatemala, mainly for women.
⊠ **Calle Matamoros 18** ☎ **(987) 70705**

Jewellery

Central Mexico

Mexico City
Bazar del Centro
Attractive jewellery emporium specialising in pearls and loose semi-precious and precious stones.
✉ Isabel la Católica 30, Centro Histórico ☎ 510 1840
🚇 Pino Suárez

Talleres de los Ballesteros
Jewellery, tableware and other decorative items in sterling silver.
✉ Amberes 24, Zona Rosa
☎ 511 8281 🚇 Insurgentes

Puebla
La Bella Elena
Unusual silver and amber jewellery designs. Near the Sunday antiques market on Plazuela de los Sapos. Upstairs café-bar.
✉ Calle 6 Sur 310 ☎ (22) 420702

Taxco
Platería Linda
Vast selection of silverware and jewellery in sterling silver, 14- and 18-carat gold. Engraving by order.
✉ Plaza Borda 4 ☎ (762) 23172

Pacific Mexico

Acapulco
B & B Gold and Silver Factory
Supplier of many of Acapulco's other jewellery shops. Vast selection.
✉ Juan Sebastián El Cano 2, by Papagayo Park ☎ (74) 830441

Taxco Exporta
Wide selection of silver jewellery from Taxco, including some unique designs. Gold pieces and choice handicrafts too. Bargaining necessary.
✉ Calle La Quebrada 315 (opposite diving cliff) ☎ (74) 827165

Ixtapa-Zihuatanejo
Astrid
One of a chain of exclusive jewellery shops, with 14- and 18-carat gold, set with precious and semi-precious stones. Choice selection of silver from Taxco.
✉ Hotel Westin Brisas Ixtapa, Playa Vista Hermosa ☎ (753) 32121

The South

Huatulco
Platería Maitl
Original designs in silver jewellery.
✉ Bugambillas 601C, La Crucecita ☎ (958) 71223 Oaxaca

Oaxaca
La Bodega del Fraile
Extensive selection of jewellery and wide price range. Monte Albán Mixtec replicas, Taxco silver and more unusual local designs using semi-precious stones.
✉ Alcalá 501 ☎ (951) 64310

Jade Artesanias
Oaxacan handicrafts alongside replica jewellery and objects.
✉ García Virgil 703 ☎ (951) 60519

Oro de Monte Albán
Fabulous display of gold jewellery reproductions of the Mixtec hoard found at Monte Albán. Fine craftsmanship using lost-wax method. Several outlets.
✉ Alcalá 403 ☎ (951) 43813

Sterling Silver
Nearly all sterling silver jewellery and tableware sold throughout Mexico originates in Taxco, so this is where you will find the best prices if you bargain hard. By law, sterling silver must be stamped '.925' which refers to the silver content of the alloy. Always shop around first before buying a particular item, and don't believe that bargains are necessarily found at street stalls.

Children's Attractions

Kids' Outings
The obvious places to take children in Mexico are the beach resorts, where there are endless facilities to keep them happy. Acapulco and Cancún offer the greatest variety, and some hotels give free accommodation to children under 12 if sleeping with their parents. Apart from the places listed, look out for shopping plazas, where video games are usually a standing fixture.

Central Mexico

Mexico City
Feria de Chapultepec
Popular amusement park with over 50 heart-stopping rides, including Mexico's only roller-coaster. Take the 'boat trip' down an artificial winding river. Avoid weekends, when queues are long.

⊠ Circuito Bosque de Chapultepec, 2nd section ☎ 230 2112 🕐 Tue–Fri 11–7, Sat–Sun 10–8 🚇 Constituyentes

Museo Papalote
A big hit with children and adults as the 250 high-tech exhibits are all interactive. IMAX auditorium shows films on Mexican culture, archaeology and other topics. Located in the second section of Chapultepec park.

⊠ Avenida Constituyentes, Bosque de Chapultepec ☎ 224 1260 🕐 Daily 9–1, 2–6, Thu 7–11PM 🚇 Constituyentes

El Nuevo Reino Aventura
Southern Mexico City's answer to Disneyland, with over 45 rides, games, a dinosaur show and other attractions.

⊠ Carretera Picacho – Ajusto 1500 ☎ 645 0559 🕐 Tue–Thu 10–6, Fri–Sun 10–7 🚇 Taxqueña or Universidad, then taxi

Zoológico de Chapultepec
Spread over 17 hectares , this zoo is home to over 1,600 animals from 270 species. Started by the Aztecs, so claims to be the world's oldest zoo.

⊠ Paseo de la Reforma, Bosque de Chapultepec ☎ 553 6229 🕐 Tue–Sun 9–4:15 🚇 Auditorio

Puebla
Africam
Impressive project that re-creates the environment of Africa to preserve and breed endangered species. Lions, tigers, giraffes, rhinos, monkeys and flamingos can be seen from your own car or park vehicles. Children's zoo and restaurant.

⊠ Km 16.5, Carretera Valsequillo 🕐 Daily 10–5 🚌 Bus 72 from Boulevard Heroes del 5 de Mayo, Puebla

Pacific Mexico

Acapulco
Castillo del Rey Leon
New recreation centre with pools and small zoo.

⊠ Carretera Pie de la Cuesta, La Barra de Coyuca ☎ (74) 810192 🕐 Daily 9–7

CICI
Aquariums, dolphins and water rides keep children more than happy at this well-established park.

⊠ Costera Miguel Alemán ☎ (74) 841960 🕐 Daily 9–7

Magico Mundo Marino
Combined aquarium and beach club on tiny island off Playa Caleta. Sharks, piranhas, stingrays all visible. Pool with water chute, seal shows.

⊠ Isla Yerbabuena ☎ (74) 831193/831215 🕐 Daily 9–7

Mazatlán
Acuario Mazatlán
Over 50 aquariums with 200 species of fish from all over the world, performing sea lions, botanical gardens, a marine museum and theatre.

⊠ Avenida de los Desportes 111, behind Motel del Sol ☎ (69) 817815/17 🕐 Daily 9:30–6

The South

Tuxtla Gutiérrez
Zoológico Miguel Álvarez del Toro
Fabulous zoo where over 200 Central American species roam in large, natural enclosures. Jaguars, quetzals, tapirs, toucans and more. All in 100 hectares of semi-tropical jungle, on the outskirts of Tuxtla. A pleasant, shady escape from the city.
✉ Off Libramiento Sur Oriente
☎ (961) 23754 🕐 Tue–Sun 8:30–5:30

Veracruz
Acuario de Veracruz
Fabulous array of tropical fish in large underwater viewing tank. Sharks and more.
✉ Villa del Mar, Boulevard Ávila Camacho ☎ (29) 327984
🕐 Daily 10–7

Villahermosa
Yumka
Huge jungle and wetlands park with 30-minute boat tour or train through African-type savanna. Good wildlife and children's facilities.
✉ Camino a Yumka, 16km from Villahermosa ☎ (93) 560107
🕐 Daily 9–5

The Yucatán Peninsula

Cancún and Tulum Corridor
Aqua Fun
Marina offering sailing lessons, diving and snorkelling, jet-skis, canoes and waverunners.
✉ Boulevard Kukulcán Km 16.5, Cancún ☎ (98) 852930
🕐 Daily 8–5

Aquaworld
Cancún's largest water-sports centre boasts an underwater 'sub see explorer' that glides through coral reefs for a dry close-up of marine life. Also jungle tours, snorkelling and diving lessons.
✉ Boulevard Kukulcán, Km 15, opposite Melia Hotel, Cancún
☎ (98) 852288 🕐 Daily 8AM–10PM

Crocosun
Small zoo 2km north of Puerto Morelos, where visitors can pet or carry animals. The 300 crocodiles are the highlight, besides spider monkeys, white-tailed deer and Mexican hairless dogs. Includes coffee shop, restaurant and gift shop.
✉ Carretera Cancún-Tulum Km 300 ☎ (98) 844782
🕐 Daily 8:30–5:30

Wet 'n Wild
Toboggans, water slides, waterchutes and several pools designed for young children. Snorkelling and diving, restaurants, bars and shops.
✉ Boulevard Kukulcán km 25, Cancún ☎ (98) 851855
🕐 Daily from 9AM

Xcaret
Vast seaside development with endless attractions, from Mayan temples to underground rivers, aquarium, swimming with dolphins, horse riding, aviary, butterfly pavilion, orchid farm and museum.
✉ 8km south of Playa del Carmen, on Highway 307
☎ (98) 730900 🕐 Mon–Sat 8:30–8:30, Sun 8:30–5 (later in summer months)

Isla Mujeres
Dolphin Discovery
Swim with dolphins on Isla Mujeres. Well organised but reservations essential. Minimum age 8 years if accompanied by adult, 12 years if not. Day trips from Cancún.
✉ Villa Pirata, Fraccionamiento Sacc Bajo
☎ (987) 70207; in Cancún (98) 830779 🕐 Four swims daily at 9, 11, 1 and 3

Swimming with Dolphins
The Dolphin Discovery Centre in Isla Mujeres has been so successful (more so with adults than children) that it has now expanded its operation to two other Yucatán sites. The largest is in Cozumel, at Laguna Chankanab, where 12 dolphins await play friends, and a second is at Puerto Aventuras (half-way between Playa del Carmen and Tulum), where four dolphins have been trained to dance and perform their astonishing acrobatics (petting permitted).

111

Nightspots & Shows

Night Culture
Apart from the beach resorts and Mexico City, the rest of the country is not the liveliest place to be in the small hours. However, some recompense may come in the form of local festivals, when brass bands suddenly strike up at 5AM, or in dance and music festivals. All towns have a Casa de Cultura, which will provide information on any upcoming local festivities.

Central Mexico

Mexico City
Ballet Folklórico
Spellbinding panorama of Mexico's diverse traditional dance, music and costumes from Aztec times to today's fiestas. The best opportunity to witness the country's rich performing arts heritage in one fell swoop. Tickets through hotels or Ticketmaster.
- ✉ **Palacio de Bellas Artes** ☎ **512 3633/529 0509. Ticketmaster 325 9000** 🕐 **Wed and Sun 8:30PM, Sun 9:30AM** 🚇 **Bellas Artes**

Bar León
Large dance hall with live bands beating out tropical sounds till late. Gets very crowded. Fun, young.
- ✉ **Calle Brasil 5, Centro Histórico** ☎ **510 3093** 🕐 **Mon–Sat 9PM–3AM** 🚇 **Zócalo**

Bar Mata
Bar on third and top-floor terrace of historical building. An old favourite for late drinks.
- ✉ **Filomena Mata 11, corner 5 de Mayo, Centro Histórico** ☎ **518 0237** 🕐 **Tue–Sun 8PM–2AM** 🚇 **Bellas Artes**

The North and Baja California

Los Cabos
Hard Rock Café
Legendary restaurant and night spot originating in London. Rock memorabilia, international dishes, live bands and a hot atmosphere.
- ✉ **Centro Comercial Plaza Bonita, Boulevard Marina, Cabo San Lucas** ☎ **(114) 33779** 🕐 **Noon–sunrise**

Iguana Bar & Restaurant
Fun, casual place in central San José. Tex-Mex food, dancing waiters, sharp *margaritas*. From 10PM a DJ or live music takes over.
- ✉ **Paseo Mijares 8, San José del Cabo** ☎ **(114) 20266** 🕐 **11AM–1AM**

Pacific Mexico

Acapulco
Baby'O
Groundbreaking night-spot with dance floor surrounded by tiered spectator seats. Latest sound and light equipment, fast-paced.
- ✉ **Costera Miguel Alemán 22, near Hyatt Regency** ☎ **(74) 847474** 🕐 **Daily from 10:30PM**

Palladium
The latest night spot in Acapulco, high on hill top. Glass walls give stunning bay views. Techno music dominates.
- ✉ **Carretera Escénica Las Brisas** ☎ **(74) 810300**

Salon Q
Hot tropical sounds keep the rhythm going in this huge dance spot with live bands. *Salsa, cumbia, merengue* and other Latin beats.
- ✉ **Costera Miguel Alemán 23, near La Palapa** ☎ **(74) 843252**

Ixtapa-Zihuatanejo
Carlos n' Charlies
Typical resort chain restaurant with lively atmosphere, loud music and dancing.
- ✉ **Boulevard Ixtapa, next to Hotel Posada Real** ☎ **(755) 30085**

La Valentina
More sophisticated than most, but still plenty of atmosphere.

✉ Boulevard Ixtapa ☎ (755) 31250

Puerto Vallarta
Cactus
Spectacular and popular nightclub in Old Vallarta.
✉ Ignacio L Vallarta 399
☎ (322) 26077

Christine's
Classic mainstream disco with wide-ranging music.
✉ Hotel Krystal Vallarta, Zona Hotelera ☎ (322) 40202 🕐 Daily 10PM–4AM

Collage
Entertainment centre with billiards and backgammon, video games, sushi bar and dance floor.
✉ Calle Proa, at entrance to Marina Vallarta ☎ (322) 10861
🕐 Daily 11AM–4AM

Zoo
Central Vallarta's most popular young night spot, easily identified by the giraffe on its roof overlooking the bay. Techno, reggae, house and disco music. Hard Rock Café is two doors away.
✉ Paseo Díaz Ordáz 630
☎ (322) 24945

The South

Huatulco
Magic Circus Disco Club
Domed dance floor attached to Hotel Marlin at western end of Santa Cruz. Mainly international rock. Live bands.
✉ Andador Huatulco 102, Santa Cruz ☎ (958) 70017
🕐 Thu–Sat nights

Mágico Trópico
Live tropical and Latino music – *salsa* and more.
✉ Gardenia 311 Altos, opposite Hotel Flamboyant
☎ (958) 70702

Poison
Hip nightclub up a dirt road behind the marina. Partly open-air.

✉ Bahía de Santa Cruz
☎ (958) 71530

The Yucatán Peninsula

Cancún
La Boom
One of Cancún's favourite night spots. Vast disco and adjacent bar, live rock.
✉ Paseo Kukulcán, near bridge ☎ (98) 831152

Cancún Queen
Paddle-steamer cruise through mangroves of Nichupté Lagoon with three-course dinner, live band, dancing and games.
✉ Aquaworld, Boulevard Kukulcán 15 ☎ (98) 85228
🕐 Daily at 6:30PM

Dady'O
Gigantic and legendary disco with tiered seating, blinding laser shows and mainly techno rhythms.
✉ Paseo Kukulcán Km 9.5
☎ (98) 833333 🕐 Daily from 9:30PM

Mango Tango
Caribbean exuberance in nightly floor show and sounds.
✉ Boulevard Kukulcán 14.2, opposite Ritz-Carlton Hotel ☎ (98) 850303 🕐 Dinner show starts at 8PM daily

Pat O'Brian's
An offspring of the well-known New Orleans bar. Lagoon view, generous drinks, outrageous setting and lots of live piano.
✉ Plaza Flamingo ☎ (98) 830418 🕐 Daily 11AM–12:30AM

Roots
Popular restaurant-bar in downtown Cancún with live jazz and blues bands on Thu, Fri and Sun night. Sat night is flamenco time with dancers and guitarists.
✉ Tulipanes 26 ☎ (98) 842437

Dady'O
Cancún's trail-blazing disco has spawned many a follower in other resorts. But it is only here that you will experience 21st-century technology in sound and light systems that some say are the best in the Americas. The nightly three-dimensional laser shows are just a kick-off. If you are in Cancún, don't miss it.

Sports

***Cenote* diving**

This rapidly expanding sport offers an alternative to the depths of the turquoise Caribbean. The limestone shelf of the Yucatán peninsula is riddled with waterways and caverns opening into *cenotes* (sinkholes). Although these are now targeted by diving outfits, remember that *cenote* diving is a dangerous sport and people have lost their lives in the underground labyrinth. Do not attempt this without a guide.

Central Mexico

Mexico City
Fiesta Charra
Mexico's exciting rodeo. The *charread* features horsemanship and lassoing skills.
✉ **Rancho del Charro, Avenida Constituyentes 500, Bosque de Chapultepec** ☎ **277 8706**
🕐 **Sun noon**
🚇 **Constituyentes**

Guadalajara
Expediciones México Verde
Experienced white water rafting agency with expeditions all over Mexico. River-rafting season coincides with rains (Jun–Oct).
✉ **José Maria Vigil 2406, Colonia Italia Providencia, 44610 Guadalajara** ☎ **(3) 641 5598/0093**

Jalapa
Amigos del Río
White water rafting at all levels in the lush tropical surroundings of the state of Veracruz.
✉ **Calle Chilpancingo 205, Colonia Progreso, 91130 Jalapa** ☎ **(28) 158817**

The North and Baja California

Los Cabos
Cabo Aquadeportes
Scuba diving, equiment rental, instructors.
✉ **Hacienda Hotel and Playa Chilena, Cabo San Lucas** ☎ **(114) 30117**

Pisces Water Sport Centre
Waterskiing, jet-ski, windsurfing, banana boats. Snorkelling trips.
✉ **Club Cascadas Beach, Cabo San Lucas** ☎ **(114) 31288**

Solmar Fleet
Sport fishing fleet with professional crews and all fishing equipment. Accommodates between three and ten people.
✉ **Solmar Hotel Desk, Cabo San Lucas** ☎ **(114) 30022, fax: 30410**

Pacific Mexico

Acapulco
Villa Vera Racquet Club
Acapulco's most famous spot for tennis, to see and be seen.
✉ **Lomas del Mar 35, Fracc Club Deportivo** ☎ **(74) 847949**

Ixtapa-Zihuatanejo
Yates del Sol
Speedboat and yacht rental, waterskiing, sunset cruises, snorkelling trips.
✉ **Zihuatanejo** ☎ **(755) 42694/43589**

Zihuatanejo Scuba Center
Wide range of diving facilities from beginners to certification courses. Night dives. Marine biologist on call for specialists.
✉ **Calle Cuauhtémoc 3, Zihuatanejo** ☎ **(755) 42147**

Puerto Vallarta
Ecogrupos
Kayaking, horse riding, bird-watching, mountain biking, whale-watching, trekking.
✉ **Ignacio L Vallarta 243** ☎ **(322) 26606**

Expediciones Cielo Abierto
Wide range of daily adventure trips including kayaking around lagoons and bays, hiking through mountain forest, birdwatching. Whale-watching Dec–Mar.
✉ **Guerrero 339, Centro** ☎ **(322) 23310, fax: 32407**

Pacific Scuba
Diving (PADI certificates) includes night dives, snorkelling at Majahuita beach, Islas Marietas and Los Arcos. Whale-watching.
✉ Juárez 722 ☎ (322) 24741

The South

Huatulco
Eco-Discover Tours
Adventure trips round Huatulco's bays. Mountain biking, scuba diving.
✉ Plaza Las Conchas L-6, Tangolunda ☎ (958) 70678

Jungle Tour
Four-wheel motor bike (ATV) tours of the jungle, ending with lunch on a beach.
✉ Lobby of Hotel Royal Maeva, Tangolunda ☎ (958) 10000 ext 729

Oaxaca
San Felipe Riding Club
Horseback expeditions into the remote mountains of Sierra Madre in small groups, with Mezcal-tasting thrown in. English and Spanish spoken.
✉ Aptdo 252, Oaxaca ☎ (951) 56864

Sociedad Cooperativa Museos Communitarios
A great opportunity to enter the heart of rural communities, on accompanied walking tours to San José el Mogote, Santa Ana del Valle or Teotitlán. Each trip includes crafts demonstrations, lunch and entrance to village museums.
✉ Tinoco y Palacios 311, Office No 16 ☎ (951) 65786 (and fax)

Veracruz
Centro de Buceo Curazao
Dive shop that rents gear and organises trips. Also handles windsurfing and sport fishing.
✉ Boca del Rio ☎ (29) 222033

Iguana Expediciones
Rafting, kayaking and scuba diving in the Veracruz area.
✉ Cotaxtla Sur 16, Colonia Petrolera, Boca del Rio ☎ (29) 211550

The Yucatán Peninsula

Cancún
Blue Peace
Scuba diving and snorkelling round coral reefs and in *cenotes*.
✉ Boulevard Kukulcán Km 16.2 ☎ (98) 8451447

Eco-Colors
American-owned adventure tour company. Snorkelling and diving trips, lagoon and jungle trips, tours of Sian Ka'an. One, three or seven days.
✉ E-mail: ecoco @cancun.rce.com.mx ☎ (98) 84950/807437

Cozumel
Diving Adventures
Scuba diving school, full PADI certficates. Daily boat dives for all levels. Nitrox dives available.
✉ Calle 5 No 2, San Miguel ☎ (987) 23009

Isla Mujeres
Coral Scuba Dive Center
Scuba diving trips, snorkelling.
✉ Avenida Matamoros 13A ☎ (987) 70763

Playa del Carmen
Skydive
Airborne thrills sky diving over the Caribbean with US certified instructor.
✉ Plaza Marina, Local 32 ☎ (987) 30192

Tulum
Tak-Be-Ha
Cavern diving, cave and *cenote* snorkelling, jungle treks.
✉ Highway 307, 1km south of Xel-Ha ☎ (987) 12092

The Great Maya Reef
Judged to be the world's second largest coral reef after Australia's Great Barrier Reef, the Great Maya Reef extends from Isla Mujeres south to the waters off Belize. This provides endless and fabulous diving and snorkelling opportunities, from Manchones and the Sleeping Sharks' Cave off Isla Mujeres, to sunken galleons off Akumal and Cozumel's staggering drop-offs and coral-covered tunnels.

What's On When

Fiesta!

Mexico's calendar is not only peppered with national festivals but also with more localised celebrations that may honour a patron saint, an agricultural activity, a seasonal change or re-enact pre-Hispanic rituals. If you can find accommodation during any of the major events, you will witness a colourful, noisy and exuberant side of the Mexican character.

* National public holidays when banks and administrative offices close.

January
1 Jan* – New Year's Day.
6 Jan – Epiphany (Three Kings' Day), celebrated with a special cake.

February
2 Feb – Día de la Candelaria.
5 Feb* – Constitution Day. Shrovetide Carnivals, above all in Veracruz and Mazatlán.

March
21 Mar* – Birthday of Benito Juárez.
21 Mar – Spring Equinox festival in Chichén Itzá.
Easter – Palm Sunday*, Maundy Thursday, Good Friday and Easter Sunday* are the big days. Taxco and the Sierra Tarahumara see the greatest celebrations. Feria de las Flores (flower festival) in Xochimilco on Easter Sunday.

April
San Marcos National Fair in Aguascalientes with *mariachis*, bullfights, rodeos. Late April to early May – varying dates.

May
1 May* – Labour Day.
5 May* – Battle of Puebla (best in Puebla itself). Cancún International Jazz Festival. Varying dates. Acapulco Music Festival. Varying dates.

June
Feast of Corpus Christi in Mexico City. Varying dates.
29 Jun – Tlaquepaque Festival in Guadalajara. *Mariachis*, dances, parades.

July
Third and last Mondays in July – Guelaguetza Festival in Oaxaca. Music and traditional dances by all Oaxaca's indigenous groups.

August
15 Aug – Assumption Day. Streets of Huamantla, Tlaxcala are carpeted with flower-petal designs. Mexico City Cultural Festival. Varying dates.

September
15, 16 Sep* – Independence Day. Military parades and festivities nationwide. President's *grito* on Mexico City's Zócalo.
21 Sep – Autumn Equinox Festival at Chichén Itzá.

October
12 Oct* – Día de la Raza (Columbus Day).
Mid- to late-Oct – Cervantino Festival in Guanajuato. Fiestas de Octubre in Guadalajara. Month-long celebrations with dance, *charreadas*, food, arts and crafts exhibits.

November
1 Nov* – Día de Todos los Santos (All Saints' Day).
2 Nov – Día de los Muertos (Day of the Dead). Mexico's fusion of pre-Hispanic and Catholic beliefs comes to the fore. Renowned celebrations at Pátzcuaro, Mixquic, Milpa Alta, Iguala. American-style Halloween is now making inroads on 31 Oct.
20 Nov* – Day of the Revolution.

December
12 Dec – Festival of the much-revered Virgen de Guadalupe. Especially celebrated at the Basílica de Guadalupe, Mexico City.
25 Dec* – Christmas Day.

Practical Matters

Above: *a shady path in San José del Cabo*
Right: *siesta-time, amigo!*

TIME DIFFERENCES

GMT
12 noon

Mexico City
← **6AM**

Germany
→ **1PM**

USA (NY)
← **7AM**

Netherlands
→ **1PM**

Spain
→ **1PM**

BEFORE YOU GO

WHAT YOU NEED

● Required
○ Suggested
▲ Not required

	UK	Germany	USA	Netherlands	Spain
Passport/National Identity Card	●	●	●	●	●
Visa	▲	▲	▲	▲	▲
Tourist Card	●	●	●	●	●
Return Ticket	▲	▲	▲	▲	▲
Health Inoculations	▲	▲	▲	▲	▲
Travel Insurance	●	●	●	●	●
Driving Licence (National)	●	●	●	●	●
Car Insurance Certificate (pay extra daily fee for CDW)	○	○	○	○	○
Car registration document	●	●	●	●	●

WHEN TO GO

Mexico City/Mexico

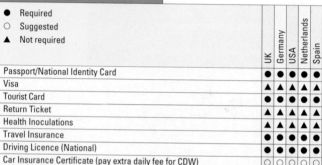

High season

Low season

19°C	21°C	24°C	26°C	24°C	23°C	23°C	23°C	23°C	21°C	20°C	19°C
JAN	FEB	MAR	APR	MAY	JUN	JUL	AUG	SEP	OCT	NOV	DEC

☀ Sun   ☁ Wet   🌦 Sunshine & showers

TOURIST OFFICES

In the UK
Mexican Ministry of
Tourism
60 Trafalgar Square,
London WC2N 5DS
☎ 0171 734 1058
Information line:
0891 600230

In the USA
Mexican Ministry of
Tourism
405 Park Avenue
Suite 1402
New York, NY 10022
☎ 212 421 6655
Information line:
1-800 446 3942

POLICE, FIRE AND AMBULANCE 080

GREEN ANGELS (Tourist patrol) (5) 250 8221

For other crisis lines, see local phone book.

WHEN YOU ARE THERE

ARRIVING

Visitors flying into Mexico have the choice between Mexico City and international airports at beach resorts such as Cancún, Los Cabos, Acapulco or Puerto Vallarta. Guadalajara and Puebla are increasingly popular alternatives. All have money-changing facilities, taxis, restaurants and duty-free shops.

Mexico City Airport
Kilometres to city centre

13 kilometres

Journey Times

🚇	20–40 minutes
🚆	N/A
🚌	30–40 minutes

Cancún Airport
Kilometres to city centre

16 kilometres

Journey times

🚇	N/A
🚆	30 minutes
🚌	20 minutes

MONEY

The monetary unit of Mexico is the peso ($), divided into 100 centavos. Coins come in 10c, 20c, 50c, $1, $2, $5 and $10 denominations. Notes are in $10, $20, $50, $100, $200 and $500. Major credit cards (particularly Visa and MasterCard) are accepted at large hotels, restaurants, travel agents and shops. Cash machines are widespread, even in small towns. International airports all have money-changing facilities with good rates.

TIME

Mexico has four time zones. Most of the country runs on Central Standard Time (6 hours behind GMT). The northern states of Nayarit, Sinaloa, Sonora and Baja California Sur are on Mountain Standard Time (7 hours behind GMT). Baja California Norte is on Pacific Standard Time (8 hours behind GMT). Quintana Roo (Cancún) is one hour ahead of Central Standard Time. All regions change their clocks in April and October.

CUSTOMS

YES

Incoming travellers can bring personal photographic, radio and sports equipment up to a value of US$300, 3 litres of spirits, 400 cigarettes, perfume, 12 rolls of film or video cassettes, and unlimited foreign currency. A completed customs form must be handed to customs officials and a button pushed: if the red light flashes you are searched, if it is green you pass through.

NO

Narcotics, weapons, protected wildlife. There are also strict regulations protecting the export of archaeological pieces.

EMBASSIES AND CONSULATES

UK
(5) 207 2149

Germany
(5) 283 2200

USA
(5) 211 0042

Netherlands
(5) 202 8453

Spain
(5) 282 2974

WHEN YOU ARE THERE

TOURIST OFFICES

**Major state tourist offices
SECTUR**
- Avenida Presidente
  Masaryk 172, Bosque de
  Chapultepec, 11587 Mexico
  DF
  ☎ (5) 255 3112/ 1006

- **Baja California Sur**
  Coordinación General de
  Turismo, Carretera
  Transpeninsular Km 5.5,
  Edificio Fidepaz, Apdo
  Postal 419, 23090 La Paz,
  Baja California Sur
  ☎ (112) 40199/40424

- **Chiapas**
  Secretaría de Desarollo
  Turístico
  Blvd Belisario Domínguez
  950, 29000 Tuxtla Gutiérrez,
  Chiapas
  ☎ (961) 24535/ 39396

- **Guerrero**
  Secretaría de Fomento
  Turístico
  Costera Miguel Alemán
  187, 35359 Acapulco,
  Guerrero
  ☎ (74) 869167/ 869171

- **Oaxaca**
  Secretaría de Desarollo
  Turístico
  Avenida Independencia
  607, Centro, 68000 Oaxaca,
  Oaxaca
  ☎ (951) 42136/ 60717

- **Yucatán**
  Departamento de Turismo
  Calle 59 No 514, Centro,
  97000 Mérida, Yucatán
  ☎ (99) 239568/ 286547

NATIONAL HOLIDAYS

J	F	M	A	M	J	J	A	S	O	N	D
1	1	1(1)	(1)	2					1	1	2	2

Jan 1	New Year's Day
Feb 5	Constitution Day
Mar 21	Benito Juárez Day
Mar/Apr	Easter (Maundy Thursday, Good Friday, Easter Sunday)
May 1	Labour Day
May 5	Battle of Puebla
Sep 16	Independence Day (starting eve of 15)
Oct 12	Columbus Day
Nov 2	Day of the Dead
Nov 20	Revolution Day
Dec 12	Festival of the Virgen de Guadalupe
Dec 25	Christmas

OPENING HOURS

○ Shops   ● Casa de Cambio
● Offices   ● Museums/Monuments
● Banks   ● Pharmacies

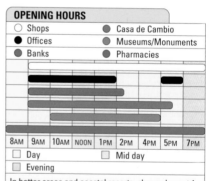

8AM	9AM	10AM	NOON	1PM	2PM	4PM	5PM	7PM

☐ Day   ☐ Mid day
☐ Evening

In hotter areas and coastal resorts, shops close at 1
or 2 for lunch, reopening at 4–5PM and finally closing
around 9PM.

Certain banks operate longer hours than above.

Post offices open Monday to Friday 8AM–6PM.

Street markets start at 7AM.

Museums are generally closed on Mondays, and
there are regional variations to the opening hours.

DRIVE ON THE RIGHT

TOILETS FREE or $1

PUBLIC TRANSPORT

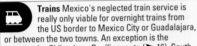

Internal Flights Domestic and regional airlines in Mexico are not cheap. Aeromexico, Mexicana and Taesa have the best schedules and deal with bookings for smaller airlines. Mexicana's Mexipass and Mayapass offer considerable savings if bought in your home country.

Trains Mexico's neglected train service is really only viable for overnight trains from the US border to Mexico City or Guadalajara, or between the two towns. An exception is the spectacular Chihuahua–Pacífico route (► 16). South of the capital, trains are slow, dirty and dangerous.

Buses The best way of seeing Mexico on a budget. *Primera* (first-class) long-distance bus services are excellent value. Each large town has a *Central Camionera* (bus station) with private lines operating different schedules and routes. For trips over 5–6 hours or during public holidays, buy your ticket a day or so in advance.

Ferries The Mar de Cortés has three ferry routes: La Paz–Mazatlán; Santa Rosalía–Guaymas; La Paz–Topolobampo. For information ☎ toll-free 01 800 696 9600. The Yucatán peninsula has boats from Playa del Carmen to Cozumel, and Puerto Juárez, Punta Sam (car ferry) or Cancún to Isla Mujeres.

Urban Transport Mexico City's metro is excellent and cheap. *Pesero* buses have their destination marked in front: fares are paid to the driver. Elsewhere in Mexico buses and *colectivos* (collective taxis) are easily available, although each city operates different identification systems. Keep small change handy for fares.

CAR RENTAL

International airports have a large choice of car rental companies. Rates vary considerably. In high season (Dec–Mar) it may be cheaper to pre-book from home. A credit card is required to make a deposit. Check the car before signing the contract.

TAXIS

Mexico City and nearby towns use meters. Elsewhere, a flat fare is charged or price negotiated in advance. Airport taxis and *colectivos* are expensive. At night in Mexico City, use radio-taxi services (☎ 519 7690/6020); taxi-muggings are common.

DRIVING

Speed limit on highways: **110kph**

Speed limit on country roads: **80kph**

Speed limit in towns: **60kph**

Compulsory for front seats.

Breath testing is not yet developed in Mexico. Due to widespread drinking, as well as hazards such as cattle and speed-breakers, it is not advisable to drive at night.

Petrol is Nova (leaded) or Magna Sin (unleaded) and is sold by the litre. Pemex (Mexican petrol) stations are plentiful in central Mexico, but fill up at every opportunity when driving in less populated areas. Payment is in cash. Petrol stations close by 10PM.

For any breakdown anywhere in Mexico, contact the Angeles Verdes (Green Angels). This unique service is free and provides on-the-spot technical assistance or tows. Every state has an Angeles Verdes Hotline so it is advisable to obtain this before setting off.

PERSONAL SAFETY

Sensible precautions should be taken, above all in larger cities. Pickpockets operate in crowded areas such as markets and bus stations, so do not tempt them by exhibiting jewellery, cameras or thick wallets. Do not leave valuables lying around in your hotel room: use a safety deposit box. Muggings are on the increase in Mexico City (► 121, Taxis) so do not carry anything other than essentials. Elsewhere, avoid taking solitary walks in remote areas or driving after dark. If anything is stolen, report it for insurance purposes.

Police assistance:
☎ **080**
from any call box

TELEPHONES

If possible, bring your own international phone card from home with access number for Mexico. Otherwise, Ladatel (long-distance) booths are easily found and operate with phone cards (30 pesos, 50 pesos, 100 pesos) bought at local stores. Ladatel offices with operators are also widespread. Avoid making long-distance calls from hotels; taxes increase costs.

International Dialling Codes

From Mexico to:

UK:	**00 44**
Germany:	**00 49**
USA & Canada:	**00 1**
Netherlands:	**00 31**
Spain:	**00 34**

POST

Correos (post offices) are in every town centre and open Mon–Fri 8–6. Overseas mail is slow but generally reliable, and is a better service than internal post. New red post-boxes (*buzón*) are now appearing, although it is safer to post letters at a post office. For anything urgent or of value, use a courier service.

ELECTRICITY

The power supply is 110 volts.
Sockets use two-flat-pin plugs (US style), so Europeans need an adaptor and transformer. Most mid- and upper-range hotels have universal outlets for shavers.

TIPS/GRATUITIES

Yes ✓ No ✗		
Restaurants (service not inc)	✓	10–15%
Cafés/bar	✓	10%
Taxis	✗	
Tour guides	✓	5–10%
Hairdressers	✓	10%
Chambermaids	✓	US$1 per day
Hotel porters	✓	US$1–2
Cloakroom attendants/toilets	✓	$1 (peso)
Petrol-pump attendants	✓	a few pesos

PHOTOGRAPHY
What to photograph: Sierra, cacti, dramatic cliffs, canyons, colonial architecture (do not use flash inside churches), market scenes. Do not photograph the sensitive and troubled indigenous people of Chiapas.
When to photograph: Mexico's clear light at higher altitudes creates strong contrasts. Early morning and late afternoon offer the best light, depending on the quality of your camera.
Where to buy film: Colour-print film and processing is widely available. Check expiry dates. Slide film is more difficult to obtain, so stock up in the cities.

HEALTH

Insurance
It is essential to take out a reliable travel insurance policy before leaving home as emergency hospital treatment can be very expensive. For minor ailments pharmacists give good advice, or you can contact a local doctor through your hotel.

Dental Services
Mexican dentists have a very good reputation. If you need emergency treatment, ask at your hotel for a recommendation.

Sun Advice
As in any semi-tropical country, sunburn is an obvious hazard. Do not sunbathe between noon and 3PM and always use a high-factor sun cream. When visiting archaeological sites, wear a hat.

Drugs
Prescription and non-prescription drugs are available from pharmacies (*farmacia*). Bring a basic first-aid kit: mosquito repellent, anti-histamine cream for insect bites, a general antibiotic, pain-relief tablets. Anti-malarial treatment need only be taken if travelling extensively in the rainy season (Jun–Sep) near swamps or lagoons.

Safe Water and Food
Never drink tapwater. *Agua purificada* (purified water) or bottled water is always supplied in hotels and bottled water is widely available. Drink plenty of water to avoid dehydration.

Food
Moctezuma's Revenge (diarrhoea) is a common traveller's complaint in Mexico. Avoid eating salads, uncooked or unpasteurised foods (watch out with ice-creams) and drinks with ice, except in decent hotels and restaurants. The liberal use of lime juice apparently acts as a deterrent against bacteria.

CONCESSIONS

Students/Youths There is little available in the way of reductions for students, as most youth discounts are for Mexican citizens. Children under 12 get reductions on domestic flights and sometimes free beds in their parents' room.

Senior Citizens Again, discounts apply solely to Mexican nationals.

CLOTHING SIZES

Mexico	UK	Europe	USA	
46	36	46	36	
48	38	48	38	
50	40	50	40	
52	42	52	42	Suits
54	44	54	44	
56	46	56	46	
41	7	41	8	
42	7.5	42	8.5	
43	8.5	43	9.5	
44	9.5	44	10.5	Shoes
45	10.5	45	11.5	
46	11	46	12	
37	14.5	37	14.5	
38	15	38	15	
39/40	15.5	39/40	15.5	
41	16	41	16	Shirts
42	16.5	42	16.5	
43	17	43	17	
36	8	34	6	
38	10	36	8	
40	12	38	10	
42	14	40	12	Dresses
44	16	42	14	
46	18	44	16	
38	4.5	38	6	
38	5	38	6.5	
39	5.5	39	7	
39	6	39	7.5	Shoes
40	6.5	40	8	
41	7	41	8.5	

WHEN DEPARTING

- Reconfirm your return flight with the airline 72 hours before departure.
- There is an airport tax on all international flights, payable at check-in in US$ or pesos, unless included in your ticket.
- Check in two hours before departure.

LANGUAGE

Spanish is the language used throughout Mexico, although in large resorts English is also widely spoken. If travelling to smaller places it is essential to know a few basic phrases. Mexican Spanish has slight differences in vocabulary and usage from Castillian Spanish, but otherwise is very similar. Accents change throughout this vast country, and in some areas you will hear local indigenous languages such as Náhuatl, Maya or Zapotec.

Do you have a single/double room?	¿Tiene una habitación sencilla/doble?
For two nights	Para dos noches
With fan/air-conditioning	Con ventilador/aire acondicionado
With double bed/twin beds	Con cama de matrimonio/dos camas
With a balcony/sea view	Con balcon/vista al mar
Is there a swimming-pool?	¿Hay una alberca?
I'd like a towel/soap/toilet-paper/blanket, please	Quisiera una toalla/jabón/papel higíenico/una manta, por favor

How much does it cost?	¿Cuánto cuesta?/Cuánta se cobre?
Very expensive/cheap/too much	Muy caro/barato/demasiado
Do you take credit cards?	¿Accepta tarjetas de crédito?
Does that include taxes?	¿Están incluidos los impuestos?
Where is the nearest exchange bureau/bank?	¿Dónde esta la casa de cambio/el banco mas cerca?
I'd like to change travellers' cheques	Quiero cambiar unos cheques de viajero
What is the exchange rate?	¿Cuál es el tipo de cambio?

Can I have the menu/bill, please?	El menu/la cuenta, por favor
We'll have two beers please	Dos cervezas por favor
A cup of black coffee (generally weak)/with milk	Un café americano/con leche
Fruit juice	Un jugo de fruta
Fizzy mineral water	Un agua mineral
A bottle of red/white wine	Una botella de vino tinto/blanco

Where is the bus station/railway-station?	¿Dónde esta el central camionera/la estación del ferrocarril?
How long is the journey?	¿Cuánto tiempo dura el viaje?
straight on/to the left/to the right	Todo derecho/a la izquierda/a la derecha
It's three blocks from here	Está a tres cuadras de aquí
How far is the nearest petrol station?	¿A qué distancia esta la gasolinera mas cerca?

Hello! Good morning	Hola! Buenos días!
Good afternoon	Buenas tardes!
Good night	Buenas noches!
Goodbye/see you	Adiós/hasta luego
Yes/no	Sí/no
Please/thank you	Por favor/gracias
It's a pleasure	De nada
Excuse me, can you help me?	¿Disculpe, me padrí ayudar?
I don't speak Spanish, I'm English (f)	No hablo español, soy inglés (a)
Do you speak English?	¿Habla inglés?
How are you?	¿Cómo está?

INDEX

Acknowledgements

The Automobile Assocation wishes to thank the following photographers, libraries and associations for their assistance in the preparation of this book:

AKG, LONDON 37; HULTON GETTY 11b, 14b; MEXICOLORE 122c (Maricela Gonzalez); MRI Banker's Guide to Foreign Currency 119; LAWSON WOOD 87b.
The remaining photographs are held in the Association's own photo library (AA PHOTO LIBRARY) and were taken by Rick Strange with the exception of the following: front cover (b) sunset and cacti, 5a, 6a, 6b, 7a, 9a, 10a, 11a, 12a, 13a, 14a, 50, 51, 52, 53, 55, 56a, 56b, 57a, 57b, 58, 59a, 59b, 64a, 68a, 117a which were taken by Robert Holmes and pages 41b, 44, 54, 62b, 70, 84b, 89b, 122a taken by Peter Wilson.

The author would like to thank the following for their assistance: the Mexican Ministry of Tourism in London, Mexico City, Oaxca and Chiapas; Mexicana Airlines, Linda Ambrosie of Tourimex and Jessica Johnson.

Page Layout: Barfoot Design

Dear Essential Traveller

**Your comments, opinions and recommendations are very
important to us. So please help us to improve our travel
guides by taking a few minutes to complete this simple
questionnaire.**

*You do not need a stamp (unless posted outside the UK). If you do not want to cut this page
from your guide, then photocopy it or write your answers on a plain sheet of paper.*

Send to: **The Editor, AA World Travel Guides,
FREEPOST SCE 4598, Basingstoke RG21 4GY.**

Your recommendations…

We always encourage readers' recommendations for restaurants, nightlife
or shopping – if your recommendation is used in the next edition of the
guide, we will send you a ***FREE* AA *Essential* Guide** of your choice.
Please state below the establishment name, location and your reasons
for recommending it.

_____

_____

_____

_____

Please send me **AA *Essential*** _____

(*see list of titles inside the front cover*)

About this guide…

Which title did you buy?
AA *Essential* _____

Where did you buy it? _____

When? m m / y y

Why did you choose an AA *Essential* Guide? _____

_____

_____

_____

_____

Did this guide meet your expectations?
Exceeded ☐ Met all ☐ Met most ☐ Fell below ☐

Please give your reasons _____

_____

_____

_____

continued on next page…

Were there any aspects of this guide that you particularly liked? _____

_____

_____

_____

Is there anything we could have done better? _____

_____

_____

_____

_____

About you...

Name (*Mr/Mrs/Ms*) _____

Address _____

_____

_____ Postcode _____

Daytime tel nos _____

Which age group are you in?

Under 25 ☐   25–34 ☐   35–44 ☐   45–54 ☐   55–64 ☐   65+ ☐

How many trips do you make a year?

Less than one ☐   One ☐   Two ☐   Three or more ☐

Are you an AA member? Yes ☐   No ☐

About your trip...

When did you book? m m / y y   When did you travel? m m / y y

How long did you stay? _____

Was it for business or leisure? _____

Did you buy any other travel guides for your trip?

If yes, which ones? _____

_____

Thank you for taking the time to complete this questionnaire. Please send it to us as soon as possible, and remember, you do not need a stamp (*unless posted outside the UK*).

Happy Holidays!